P9-DHQ-760

All Things Weird and Wonderful

Stuart Briscoe

VICTOR BOOKS

a division of SP Publications, Inc., Wheaton, Illinois
Offices also in Fullerton, California • Whitby, Ontario, Canada • London, England

Second printing, 1978

Scripture quotations are from the King James Version of the Bible.

Library of Congress Catalog Card Number: 77-075903
ISBN: 0-88207-749-X

© 1977 by SP Publications, Inc. World rights reserved
Printed in the United States of America

VICTOR BOOKS
A division of SP Publications, Inc.
P.O. Box 1825 • Wheaton, Ill. 60187

Contents

To
David, Judy, and Peter,
three young people who fill my life
with loving challenge
and vibrant Christian
excitement.

Preface

My initial interest in writing this book was sparked by the response I received from a number of people to whom I preached a brief series of messages from Ezekiel. Most of them said that they knew nothing about him or his book, but were glad to learn a little and were stimulated to further study.

There are several reasons why I believe Ezekiel is the kind of book in the Bible that most people don't read but should.

First, the book's main thrust is to show people who God really is. He repeatedly told Ezekiel that He was acting in a certain way so that people would know "I am the Lord." People don't really know the Lord today because in many of our churches we talk about ourselves and our problems more than the Lord and His requirements.

Second, Ezekiel lived in a period of societal disintegration. In this breakdown he discovered both the sinfulness of man and the hand of God and addressed himself to them. Our society is coming apart at the seams, but those who admit it seem to think the answers are political and economic rather than moral and spiritual. Ezekiel helps us understand this.

Third, I have found all kinds of people who are fascinated by the slightly weird, the occult, and the "way out" aspects of today's world! Those people really need to get alongside Ezekiel, because if God ever had a man "way out there" it was Ezekiel.

Fourth, we are a communications-crazy generation. In the Church we are getting so excited about methods of communication that we are in danger of forgetting that the message communicated must never be sacrificed at the altar of methodology. What does Ezekiel have to say to this? As one of the most gifted, unpredictable, and effective communicators of unpalatable truth in God's Book, he's an absolute must for all would-be communicators.

Fifth, in the Church of Jesus Christ we have differences. This is to be expected, but the ways we handle the differences are rather unexpected. Instead of showing our maturity by coolly discussing them, we polarize! Ezekiel gives us opportunity for improving our record!

The Book of Ezekiel is not easy to study or to understand and accept its message. It is not easy to interpret or, by any means easy to apply, but it amply rewards careful, reverent study. So follow the advice of the wise man who said, "My son, if you wilt receive my words and hide my commandments with thee, so that thou incline thine ear unto wisdom, and apply thine heart to understanding; yea, if thou criest after knowledge, and liftest up thy voice for understanding; if thou seekest her as silver and searchest for her as for hid treasures; then shalt thou understand the fear of the Lord, and find the knowledge of God" (Prov. 2:1-5). I am sure you will be enriched by your time spent in Ezekiel.

1

All Things
Slightly Strange

Ezekiel 1

Sunsets work wonders for even the most dismal places. They are God's gift to unbearable locations. Even the dustiest streets and the foulest slums are bathed in a rosy pink, golden orange wash. For a few minutes the unpleasant becomes slightly pleasant and the intolerable almost tolerable. But even the most original sunset had its work cut out to make Tel-abib look like anything other than the dismal camp for Judean exiles that it had been for five long years.

A Sad Heap

The "tell" from which the camp derived its name was a dusty mound consisting of the ruins of the towns and villages that had existed on that site and had died from natural causes or been destroyed by enemies. With each demise the sad heap got bigger, a mute testimony to the decay and destruction of the cruel years. To such a forbidding place the exiles had been directed. They had been granted permission to establish their homes and get on with the business of surviving. They had built their mud-brick houses, established some degree of order, and endeavored desperately to bring meaning to a meaningless existence. But a sad, sticky cloud of hopelessness sat on the camp as it waited quietly to be added to the heap of ruins.

Ezekiel watched the sunset as he had done hundreds of times

9

before. His eyes, however, were not focused on the sun-burnished waters of the irrigation canal they called the River Chebar or on the rolling, burning plains stretching to infinity. In the recesses of his mind he thought of Jerusalem, about 700 miles away along the rays of the sunset. To Ezekiel, the beloved city was the center of his shattered hopes, fractured plans, and the blazing barrenness of his own young life.

Fractured Plans

When Ezekiel was 20 years of age his father Buzi, a priest of the order of Zadok, had sensed that he was leaning toward the priesthood and had encouraged him to acquaint himself as much as possible with the order and service of the temple. For five years he had immersed himself in the temple and the One whom he worshiped. The mandatory 10 years which must elapse before, at 30, he could be fully initiated were not onerous at all. But the initiation never came.

In 597 B.C., when Ezekiel was 25 years of age, five years short of his goal, the Babylonian armies besieged Jerusalem and the city fell after a brief resistance. The attack was perfectly predictable because Jehoiakim had rebelled against Babylonian rule, an action which was as endearing to the Babylonians as Czechoslovakia's insurrection in 1968 was to the Soviet Union.

For over 20 years, Jeremiah the prophet had been warning the people of Jerusalem that God would judge them and that disaster was imminent. But the people didn't want to hear so they put Jeremiah in the stocks, had him flogged, and generally showed their distaste for anything that might be designed to halt their lemminglike charge toward extinction.

Rotten Figs

After the fall of Jerusalem, everybody expected the worst from the Babylonian "heathen," but things could have been much worse than they turned out. Nebuchadnezzar ordered neither mass executions nor a mass deportation. He simply skimmed off the city leadership and shipped them to Babylonia. Jeremiah explained the situation with a parable about two baskets of fruit. One was full of choice fruit and those left in Jerusalem were the rotten ones (Jer. 24).

If there was any comfort for Ezekiel in a most uncomfortable situation, it was that he was a member of the choice basket. But right now that was small comfort. To put it quite bluntly, Ezekiel was depressed. His career which should have been blossoming was withering on the vine. His beloved Jerusalem, the center of all that he held dear, was in the grip of the despised Babylonians and populated by people unable or unwilling to function as God's people in the city of God. And Tel-abib was awful.

It was particularly frustrating to Ezekiel to know that while Jerusalem was declining, Babylon was booming. Jerusalem, the place of Jehovah's dwelling, was falling apart while Babylon, the scene of idolatry and sensual excess, was beautiful. The city boasted hanging gardens, magnificent fortifications, innovative architecture, and bustling, prosperous people. In fact, look where he would, there was nothing to brighten Ezekiel's day or alleviate his gloom.

A Real Vision

That was till he looked northward. Way out on the plains the wind was blowing up a cloud of dust that swirled and grew bigger, tinged by the sunlight to a glowing, burning intensity. At least that's what he thought he saw till what he saw with his eyes began to give way to what he saw in his spirit. His 20/20 vision became 100/100 vision. He felt a real vision coming on.

It would be futile to deny that Ezekiel got himself involved in a number of weird and wonderful things. Yet, at the same time, it is probably not too helpful to put him into a psychological category as has been done by many. Stalker wrote in his commentary on Ezekiel, "Ezekiel has been called a cataleptic, a neurotic, a victim of hysteria, a psychopath, and even a definite paranoid schizophrenic, as well as being credited with powers of clairvoyance and levitation." But R. K. Harrison, in his *Introduction to the Old Testament,* wrote, "Attempts at psychiatric or psychological profundity by amateurs are serious enough in their import when foisted on their contemporaries, but when they are urged in all earnestness in connection with long-dead individuals of another culture and a different age, they become merely amusing."

So we will simply take the record at face value and see how what God had to say to Ezekiel in those days applies to what needs to be said to us in our day.

A Little Weird

Ezekiel's account of the vision is, by Western standards, a little weird! Yet it holds a strange fascination for all who read it. Not because we are all a little weird, enamored of the grotesque and curious about the strange and the absurd, but because Ezekiel said he had "visions of God" (Ezek. 1:1). To him the "heavens were opened" (1:1) and as a result, his mind was expanded to such a degree that he was introduced to dimensions of knowledge and experience far beyond anything he had known previously.

To say that the vision was timely is to make a massive understatement. Ezekiel and his contemporaries desperately needed a vision of God, as do all people whose circumstances have become their obsession and whose experience has become their dominating passion. When man's existence becomes almost totally his theme and song, society is in deep trouble. When man becomes primarily problem-oriented, when rapid solutions are his goal, when personal survival is his passion and personal comfort his life ambition, then society is on the brink of disintegration. When economics, politics, philosophies, and psychologies revolve around selfish people who become more selfish and a man's horizons stretch no further than the confines of his personal interests, one thing is necessary to restore correct perspective to life and renew right dimension to existence. A vision of God is what that society needs.

God has a major problem in granting visions to people. He knows they can't live with a vision of Him and yet they can't live without a vision of Him. So what does God do? He gradually unveils Himself. He reveals enough of Himself to convey an accurate picture but not so much that the receiver is completely overwhelmed.

The Word of the Lord

Gradually Ezekiel became aware that he was on the receiving end of a vision. There was a whirling, powerful wind that in some way produced a towering, forbidding cloud that was itself flashing with light and burning with such intensity that it looked like a glowing, burning metallic substance. He described his vision as being the means whereby "The word of the Lord came expressly to [me] . . . and the hand of the Lord was there upon [me]" (1:3). He believed that the Lord was showing Himself in the towering, whirling, burning cloud.

There was some revelation of the Being of God to Ezekiel as he observed the phenomenon. There was a sense of irresistible power in the whirlwind as it swept across the plains, gathering momentum and bending everything to its will. Perhaps Ezekiel thought of God being able to rush, like the wind, into the camp and sweep through its lowly streets, blowing on to proud Babylon and even across the desert to Jerusalem, sweeping all before Him. What a tonic to his discouraged heart to be reminded that God was still capable of moving into Tel-abib or Babylon and even Jerusalem bringing His own powerful freshness wherever He chose to move.

A Consuming Fire

The reminder that God was even more towering and majestic than the cloud was not out of place. When Ezekiel's forefathers were in the wilderness they had been reminded daily of the imposing Presence in the cloud by day and the pillar of fire by night (Ex. 13:21-22). But Ezekiel's contemporaries had no such revelation. For years they had been convinced that if their God was still around He certainly was not imposing enough to get a grip on their situation. They had come to the conclusion that their problems were considerably bigger than their God and that hopelessness was their daily diet. In addition, they certainly needed the message about the Lord being a burning, glowing God. Moses had made it quite clear that the Lord was not about to be pushed around but that He was, among other things, "a consuming fire, even a jealous God" (Deut. 4:24). The writer of the Epistle to the Hebrews picked up the idea and encouraged the readers to "have grace whereby we may serve God acceptably with reverence and godly fear; for our God is a consuming fire" (Heb. 12:28-29).

There is little doubt that the captives at Tel-abib had not only lost sight of the greatness and grandeur of their God because of the disastrous experience they were going through, but they had also forgotten that God is to be treated with great reverence and respect. The Lord refused to accept such a situation and was determined to speak to Ezekiel and through him to the people. But first Ezekiel himself had to become acutely aware of the reality of God in his own life.

Solution-Seekers

In times of national despair and societal disaster, earnest people seek real solutions to their problems. But often they fail to realize that the problems may well have deep spiritual roots and may require basic spiritual solutions. For instance, the terrible societal problems of 18th-century England were solved, to a great extent, through the preaching of John Wesley. He set himself to "reform the nation, particularly the Church, and to spread scriptural holiness over the land." But first he needed a revelation of God that would bring him to a commitment of loving reverence and deep filial service. Ezekiel saw the Lord on the plains of Chebar—Wesley in a small room in Aldersgate. As a result, both had ministries that changed the climate of their nations spiritually, politically, and socially.

Living Creatures

As Ezekiel was drawn further into the strange experience, more details began to emerge. Out of the burning cloud there appeared "four living creatures" (1:5). Each of the creatures had four faces resembling a man, a lion, an ox, and an eagle (1:10). They stood with their backs to each other; in the center of the square they formed was something that burned like coals and flashed like lamps (1:13).

Each of these creatures had four wings, two of which were stretched out to join with the wings of the next creature to form the base of a large platform on which was something resembling a throne (1:11, 26). Beside the creatures were massive wheels full of eyes! (1:18) The whole platform and throne moved with lightning speed, with a great whirring sound (1:14).

It's not surprising that in this description some UFO enthusiasts see biblical justification for their belief! But something about what Ezekiel saw shows that his visions were far greater than any UFO, for seated on the throne was "the likeness of the glory of the Lord" wrapped in a dazzling rainbow of exquisite colors (1:28). Quite a vision!

A Matter of Majesty

This remarkable revelation is aimed at showing the Lord in His majesty. The wheels, the creatures, the eyes, and the flashing coals are all fascinating and relevant, but the One seated on the throne is the focal point of the vision. Everything else is designed to illustrate some aspect of His Being and action.

I think Ezekiel must have looked at the vision rather like a small boy looks at a giraffe for the first time. Starting with what he could see from his ground level position, Ezekiel slowly lifted his gaze, taking in all the details till his neck was almost breaking off. Then he got the whole incredible picture and tried to take it in.

Four Faces

Let's start at the bottom of the picture and slowly work our way up to the Lord on His throne.

The living creatures were unlike anything known to man. John Taylor in his commentary notes that the cherub figures on the throne of King Hiram of Byblos most resemble the creatures, but even they are not particularly helpful. The most important thing about the living creatures is that they exist as part of the vehicle whereby God made Himself known.

The creatures' faces depicting man, lion, ox, and eagle were arranged so that whichever way you looked at them you could see all four. If you want to experiment, take four children's building blocks with different letters on each face and arrange them so they form a hollow square and then see how many letters you can see as you look at them from different angles. The significance of the kinds of faces is explained by the old rabbis. They said that man is the greatest of created beings, the lion the greatest among the wild animals, the ox the greatest domestic beast, and the eagle the greatest bird. Though fishes and creepy crawlies weren't mentioned, the obvious implication is that all created beings are made by God to be submissive to His control and to be the means of showing His glory.

The Servants of God

Many details are given about the living creatures and they are worth looking into briefly. Remember the purpose for which the creatures existed and you will see that their characteristics are those needed by all God's servants if they are to function adequately as the platform from which He operates. Ezekiel needed to be reminded of this because the Lord was set to do a great work through him. The vision was preparing him by showing the Lord to him and by reminding him about the things God expects to see in those whom He uses.

First, "they had the likeness of a man" (1:5) which reminds us that of all the created orders, *humanity* is the one the Lord uses primarily for His purposes.

Second, "their feet were straight feet" (1:7) which speaks of the necessity for *stability* in the work of the Lord.

Third, "they sparkled like the color of burnished brass" (1:7), a clear reference to their *purity*.

Fourth, "they had the hands of a man under their wings" (1:8), which graphically points out that the Lord's work requires people with a sense of *practicality* to go with their wings!

Fifth, "their wings were stretched upward" (1:11), which portrays a great sense of urgency and *mobility*.

Sixth, "two wings covered their bodies" (1:11), demonstrating their *humility*.

Seventh, "they went every one straight forward" (1:12) which means that they had a great sense of purpose and commitment and moved with purpose and *integrity*.

Eighth, "whither the Spirit was to go they went" (1:12) is the great statement of their *availability*.

Ninth, "their appearance was like burning coals of fire" (1:13) describes their *intensity*.

Tenth, "they ran and returned as the appearance of a flash of lightning" (1:14) gives a tremendous sense of their *activity*.

This is an awesome picture of the ministry of God. Ezekiel was being shown in glorious technicolor that God moves in our world through His created beings and that His service is both the most exhilarating and terrifying activity in which humanity can be involved.

Perhaps Ezekiel had mixed feelings at this stage. Part of him may have been saying, "Hold it. I can't take any more of this. Give me a few years to get all this squared away in my mind." But the other part would have wanted the vision to continue. "Show me more. I can't get enough of this revelation of God and His service."

Wheels

Wheels began to demand Ezekiel's attention. Perhaps they slowly came into focus as if someone were operating a zoom lens on a television camera. The creatures faded into the background and the wheels began to roll toward him. Terrifying wheels.

Most people who have never heard of the prophecy of Ezekiel have heard from the spiritual that "Ezekiel saw de wheels." But I'm not too convinced that the spiritual says what Ezekiel really saw.

Have you ever tried to parallel park a car in a limited space? Sometimes you can get the rear of the car in the space but not the front. Or you get the front end sticking out too far or the rear end on the sidewalk. Don't you think it would be great if you could have wheels with other wheels set in them at right angles? Then all you would have to do would be to draw alongside the space, put the other wheels in gear, and park the car sideways. Right in the place, to the very inch!

That's what Ezekiel's wheels were like. "Wheels in the middle of a wheel" (1:16) means that they could move in any direction at anytime, or as Ezekiel explained it, "When they went they went upon their four sides and they turned not when they went" (1:17).

He was impressed by the fact that God can get anywhere He wants to at anytime and, if necessary, move in four directions simultaneously! The technical word for what he saw is "omnipresence."

Then he noticed the size of the wheels. John Taylor points out that the literal translation of Ezekiel's words is, "As for their rims, height to them and fear to them." In other words, he was overwhelmed with the sheer size and immensity of the movement of God. Sometimes the wheels touched the earth; other times they lifted off like a helicopter and took off like a rocket. Their power was awesome. Here the technical word is "omnipotence."

Rims Full of Eyes

Perhaps the weirdest thing that Ezekiel noticed about the wheels was that the rims were "full of eyes" (1:18). George Orwell, in the novel *1984* managed to frighten many people by his portrayal of "Big Brother," who could watch what everyone was doing. But compared to Ezekiel's vision, Big Brother needs glasses. For "the eyes of the Lord run to and fro throughout the whole earth" (2 Chron. 16:9). Nothing is hidden from His view. He is aware even of thoughts and desires of people's hearts. The word for this is "omniscience."

The wheels and the creatures were motivated by a spirit. "Whithersoever the spirit was to go, they went . . . for the spirit of the living creatures was in the wheels" (Ezek. 1:20). This spirit has been interpreted differently by different people, but it would appear that the significance of the spirit in the wheels and the creatures is that God used them in His own mysterious way, touching both heaven and earth with His omnipotent, omniscient, omnipresent presence.

A Permanent Firmament

Then the "firmament" came into focus. Many scholars suggest that Ezekiel saw on top of the wheels and the creatures a kind of massive platform made of a crystallike substance that gleamed and sparkled in phenomenal variety and splendor (1:22-25).

It is interesting to note that as Ezekiel advanced into his vision he became more and more vague. The words "appearance" and "likeness" become increasingly common and it is easy to understand his problem. He was trying to describe a vision of God, which incorporated many of His divine attributes, with words that were incapable of conveying the real meaning. On top of this he was trying to grapple with the sheer overwhelming nature of what he had seen. It was as if he had heard Beethoven for the first time without any musical training and then tried to play the composer's Fifth Symphony on a tin whistle.

Flat on His Face

He saw the "likeness of a throne" and "upon the likeness of the throne was the likeness as the appearance of a man" (1:26). In addition, there was the "appearance of fire," the "appearance of loins," the "appearance of the [rainbow]" (1:27), all of which culminated in "the appearance of the likeness of the glory of God" (1:28). The One on the throne spoke from His glorious position and the voice was as the "voice of the Almighty" (1:24). And Ezekiel fell on his face. He had taken about as much as he could handle!

While he lies on his face, let's summarize what he saw and see if we need to have a similar vision of God. First, he was reminded of the *mystery of God* moving, glowing, sweeping in the cloud and the whirlwind. Is there a possibility that we have lost all sense of this mystery of God because we have tried to make God fit our needs? Then Ezekiel was alerted to the greatness of the *ministry of God,* what it really means to be called to be part of

His movement in the world. Could it be that our service today has become dull and mundane? On top of this, Ezekiel saw something of the *majesty of God,* "high and lifted up," as Isaiah explained it (Isa. 6:1). This finally brought him to his knees, which is where everyone who is going to be used of God has to begin.

2

The Strange Ways of God

Ezekiel 2:1-2

I can still remember vividly my first day as a working man. Fresh out of high school, I reported for duty, trailing the clouds of glory that my career as student leader, athlete, and student had firmly attached to me. To my dismay, I found myself unknown, unwanted, and unheeded. The people in the office were so far beyond me in experience and so superior to me in knowledge that I felt overwhelmingly inadequate, clumsy, and stupid. I didn't know whether to run, hide, scream, or collapse in a quivering heap.

Imagine how Ezekiel must have felt as he was confronted with a vision of God so brilliant and supernatural that he was incapable of coping with it. How long he lay in the desert dust we do not know. What thoughts teemed through his shattered mind we can only surmise. Lifted as he was from the mundane to the sublime, he lay powerless in the grip of inadequacy and unworthiness. He had the ultimate experience—a vivid confrontation with Almighty God.

Amused or Ashamed?
The Jewish rabbis forbade anyone under 30 years of age to read the account of the vision. Presumably they felt that it would be too much for the sensitive spirits of their young people. This may seem amusing to us, but perhaps we should be ashamed, for

we have allowed the sensitivities of our young people to be so brutalized by constant exposure to the violent and the sordid that they are capable of approaching the most overwhelming situation with nonchalance. Even God! And adult sensibilities have been so anesthetized by cynical disregard of His supernatural power, awesome purity, and utter otherness that contemporary society seems to convey the impression that nothing will shake them or move them.

The modern mind sees man as awesome and God as tiresome. If God is considered at all He is viewed from the wrong end of a telescope. Man looms large on his own horizon while God skulks in the shadows waiting to be needed. Psychology, sociology, ecology, and technology have largely replaced theology. And where theology survives it owes more to the contemporary concepts of God than to God's revelation of Himself. Today's God is not the God of Ezekiel who puts men on their faces before Him, but rather a pygmy deity who condones impotence and disgrace and conveniently adapts to the modern scene. Our society feels that God needs to learn from the modern mind that His rightful place is at the feet of man. He must languish in dismal exile while man flies his chariots to the galaxies.

The Glory of God

It is important that we notice exactly what Ezekiel saw: "the appearance of the likeness of the glory of God." Admittedly there is considerable vagueness in the statement as evidenced by the phrase "the appearance of the likeness," but there is nothing vague about "the glory of the Lord." Ezekiel knew exactly what he was seeing even though he didn't have either the mental capacity or the vocabulary to explain it adequately. The Hebrew word for *glory* means literally "weight" or "worthiness." The idea behind the word is that if a person has anything of worth, he will make it obvious, and the more substance or weight he demonstrates the more worthy he is. This is a somewhat shaky premise, but that's the way they thought. It may be that our modern status symbols betray similar thought patterns. The main point is, however, that Ezekiel was treated to a vision which demonstrated the "weight" or the "worthiness" of the Lord. He saw the things that show what God is really like and how worthy He is of His creatures' worship and adoration.

Pillar of Fire

God had shown forth His glory down through the troubled history of Ezekiel's people. In the wilderness He had continually demonstrated His glorious presence among them in the cloud by day and the pillar of fire by night (see Ex. 13:21-22). When Solomon built his temple, the glory of the Lord filled the place so mightily that the priests could no longer minister (1 Kings 8:11).

The people of Israel and their physical and spiritual descendants have been prone to lose sight of the wonder of the Lord and the necessary response of worshipful service that the knowledge of Him demands. It is this fatal tendency to forget or ignore His glory that the Lord Himself resisted all through the history of His people and still resists in our day. Ezekiel's ministry was basically a reminder to willfully forgetful people that to overlook who God is, is to invite disaster. To return to an attitude of personal acknowledgement of the Lord in all His majestic glory is to open the door to a life where that glory fills the place.

The Presence of the Lord

It is a tragic day for any individual or institution when the reality of the Lord's presence is lost and the tangible evidences of His abiding are withdrawn. I am convinced that this is what has happened in innumerable lives and countless institutions.

Many Christians are so wrapped up in themselves that they have lost any real sense of God Himself. Many churches are so oriented to cater to the improvement of people's circumstances that they tend to overlook the One whom the psalmist said was "the strength of my heart and my portion for ever" (Ps. 73:26). Some countries are proud of God in their heritage and of Christian principles in their roots, yet they so abuse the Lord by chronically neglecting or blatantly disobeying Him that they are hardly recognizable as anything other than pagan cultures.

We must join Ezekiel in the desert dust before God's revelation of Himself in order that our fantasies may be replaced by true perspective and the truth of God.

Other But Near

Theologians talk about the "transcendence" and "immanence" of God. "Transcendence" means that God is so utterly "other" and extraordinary in His being and nature that He is far above everything that we are. He's in a different league from mankind! "Immanence" refers to His closeness and involvement in the affairs of mankind and his world. It conveys the truth that even though He is beyond our comprehension and adequate appreciation, He is intimately concerned in our affairs.

When I was a boy, Stanley Matthews, the greatest soccer star of the time, lived in England. He was spoken of in hushed tones and watched by thousands of fans with a reverence that bordered on worship. Imagine my delight one day when I not only got to meet him but actually spoke to him as he signed his autograph for me. Then to add euphoria to ecstacy, the next day a national newspaper ran a picture of Stanley Matthews talking to Stuart Briscoe! I never lost my sense of wonder at his stardom, but after that day Stanley Matthews and I had something in common. We had conversed for 30 seconds and the newspaper proved it! I had experienced his "transcendence" and his "immanence."

Without a balanced understanding of God's transcendence and immanence people get into all kinds of problems. Concepts of God's remoteness lead to a sense of unrelatedness to Him which can breed a dead formalism. But those who major only on His immanence and availability to them run the risk of so minimizing His essential nature that they end up with a friend who can be treated as casually as a friend and as carelessly as an acquaintance.

Balanced Relationship

Ezekiel's experience illustrates the correct balance. Shattered by the vision of the glory of the Lord, he was not left to grovel in despair. It was not God's intention to play the bully or behave like a drill sergeant. His concern was not to make Ezekiel squirm for the rest of his days as an atonement for his inadequacies. The Lord was revealing the truth of who He really is so that Ezekiel, in an attitude of reverent, submissive worship, would be free and eager to know more of the Lord.

Ezekiel wrote, "and I heard a voice of one that spake" (1:28). The God of the whirling, whirring chariot had something to say to a cowering man! Therein lies the balance of the transcendence and immanence of God. When both are understood and the poles of irreverent casualness and cold formality are avoided, a balanced relationship incorporating the reverence due Deity and the love due a Friend becomes the norm.

Son of Man

The first recorded words of the Lord to Ezekiel were "Son of man" (2:1). It is significant that this phrase is repeated more than 90 times in the Book of Ezekiel whereas it occurs on only one other occasion in the Old Testament. While the expression has been interpreted in various ways, it is generally accepted that it refers to Ezekiel's humanness, particularly as it was evident in his frailty and limited ability. This is particularly interesting in the light of the fact that Ezekiel was no pushover. He was no tabby cat meowing in the streets of Tel-abib!

Nevertheless, in the divine reckoning he was a frail, failing creature and he would not be allowed to forget it. Yet his name Ezekiel means "God strengthens." Thus God reminded his man that in himself he was "son of man," but in the Lord he was "God strengthens."

Full of Surprises

Vast as God is, He involves Himself in details. Omnipotent as He is, He insists on employing a failing "son of man" to work out His purposes. He has access to palaces, yet chooses to visit refugee camps. Cherubim and chariots are part of His equipment, yet humanity is an integral part of His operations. His voice is like the sound of many waters, but He can speak to a man without shattering his nerves or his eardrums.

He has His own way of doing things and they are far above man's ways. Happy is the man who takes time to learn of the ways of God, falling at His feet and hearing His word.

Having put Ezekiel on his face, the Lord told him to stand on his feet (2:1). The compelling word of God became as compelling as the appearance of God. The one put him down, the other raised him up.

We may be tempted to ask God, "Why put him down if you intend to make him stand up?" But that is the way of God. He makes tall those who know how to lie low. Those who abase themselves are exalted; those who die are resurrected; those who submit are freed; those who are weak become strong. Strange, but true, and so hard for humans to learn!

Obedience

God was at once the Commander and the Performer. He *told*

Ezekiel to stand up and then *made* him stand up. This is another of those important, strange ways of God. The Lord commands His children to do the things He requires, and the only valid response to a command of God is obedience. This requires an act of the will, and nothing ever takes away the necessity for human beings to act in obedience by exercising their wills in line with God's requirements.

Even though the necessity for obedience is always present, the capacity for obedience is often lacking. Many people have assumed that because they don't have the capacity, they are released from the necessity. They say to themselves, "God knows I can't do that, so I will ignore the fact that He told me to do it." Such an attitude makes it easy to live a life of disobedience and still feel comfortable.

But disobedience is never right even if we have persuaded ourselves that we can't obey. If God commands, He demands obedience, but only because He supplies the ability to obey whenever He commands. We can obey because He enables us to do so, and if He does not enable us, He would not dream of commanding us. Ezekiel was commanded to stand when he could not, but as he obeyed the command, he found the strength available.

Fruit and Action

You are probably familiar with the list of attitudes and attributes which the Scriptures call "the fruit of the Spirit." But have you ever noticed the direct relationship between this fruit and the commands of Scripture to ensure that the fruit is evident in believers' lives? For example, Paul wrote, "the fruit of the Spirit is love" (Gal. 5:22-23). But Jesus said to His disciples, "This is my commandment, that ye love one another" (John 15:12). Taken on its own, Paul's statement may lead one to assume that since love is the fruit of the Spirit, it will grow automatically like bananas or cucumbers. But Jesus' words give the impression that love is something the Lord expects us to produce.

If love grows automatically, why did the Lord command that His disciples love? On the other hand, if disciples have the ability to love, why talk about love being the fruit of the Spirit? The answer must be that the responsibility to love is laid fairly and squarely on the disciples' shoulders but the enabling to love rests in the indwelling Holy Spirit.

Work your way through the list of "the fruit of the Spirit" found in Galatians 5 and fit the commands of Scripture to it. In case you need one more clue, compare "the fruit of the Spirit is . . . joy" (Gal. 5:22) with "rejoice in the Lord alway, and again I say rejoice" (Phil. 4:4).

The Spirit Entered

Sometimes we think that only New Testament-oriented people understand the work of the Holy Spirit in the life of the believer as He empowers for obedience. Ezekiel knew something of that as well. He said, "And the Spirit entered into me when he spake unto me and set me upon my feet" (Ezek. 2:2). He did not use the phrase "the Holy Spirit," but we know that the Spirit enabled him to obey and came as a result of hearing God's word. It is perfectly legitimate for us to see this as a reference to the work of the Holy Spirit in the life of the prophet. It was His power that enabled Ezekiel to stand as he obeyed the command.

The imparting of spiritual dynamic to Ezekiel was related to what the Lord said to him. "The Spirit entered into me *when* He spake." There was power in the word as it was received. Scripture repeatedly teaches that there is something unique about what God says. "The worlds were framed by the Word of God . . ." (Heb. 11:3) is the way the writer to the Hebrews explained the remarkable events of Creation. Genesis records "God said . . . and it was so" (1:7, 9, 11, 15, 24, 29-30). The creative energy of God is released in His dynamic utterances. The Lord Jesus insisted, "The words that I speak unto you are spirit and they are life" (John 6:63). He illustrated this conclusively in the resurrection of Lazarus. "Lazarus, come forth" was all He said, but there was enough power in those words to awaken Lazarus in the realm of the dead and bring him back to life, graveclothes and all! (John 11:43-44)

Receiving the Word

Our modern era is centuries away from the days of Ezekiel and Lazarus, but that does not alter the fact that spiritual dynamic is related to the reception of the Word of God. It is unlikely that the phenomena of God's spoken word will be demonstrated today exactly as it was in the days of Ezekiel and Lazarus. But God still speaks, and as Henry Twells wrote:

Thy touch has still its ancient power,
No word from Thee can fruitless fall.

Though the media of communication may change, the Word is still the communicator of the power of God. Though some of us may wish that we could hear a big booming word from God, we should remind ourselves that we have a much fuller revelaticn of God's truth in Scripture than was ever available to the people in bygone eras and that we need to be more aware of the spiritual power in the Scriptures than we have ever been. It is in the study of the Word of God that we are to discover the spiritual power that so many crave today.

Off-center Desiring

There is no doubt that many Christian believers seek fresh experiences with God. More and more people are demonstrating a hunger and thirst for fuller and deeper knowledge of God, yet some of the seeking and much of the desiring is off-center. This is understandable. If the way to spiritual power is through the study and assiduous application of God's Word to our lives, it is obviously going to take a considerable amount of time, effort, and discipline. But our contemporary society is so programmed to expect and demand the instant solution, the immediate answer, and ready-made maturity that believers have become infected with the same plague. There is a great interest in anything that offers or implies a quick, easy way to success, and we are producing many earnest believers who have gone through numerous exciting spiritual experiences but are still biblically illiterate. They have been led to expect spiritual power and effectiveness without taking the yoke of the Lord Jesus upon them and learning of Him. We must be wary of the means to spiritual growth that appear to do away with the necessity for the Word of God.

Power and the Word

You may be thinking, "That's fine, but I know some people who have graduated from seminary, or attend Bible-teaching churches and they are so dull and ineffectual that they make me tired. How can you suggest that spiritual power results from receiving the Word of God when there are many people who have received it and show little power or vitality?"

We can confuse biblical education with reception of the Word of God. For instance, we can learn the order of the books of the Bible and never learn how to obey one order contained in any of the books. Or we can memorize 1 Corinthians 13 and have no concept of what it means to love. I knew a girl who graduated magna cum laude from a Bible school and six months later renounced the Lord and married an unbeliever.

Receiving the Word of God means a lot more than getting it into our heads. Receiving it means acting upon it in faith and obedience. It is possible for one to have a Bible education and demonstrate little of spiritual dynamic, but it is not possible to really receive the Word of God and be devoid of spiritual power and effectiveness.

Your Reservations Are Confirmed

If you have peeked into the succeeding chapters you will have discovered that there are 48 of them, and you may be dubious about our ever getting through them. We spent all this time on the early chapters because they are so important to our understanding of the whole book and so basic to our understanding of God's ways with His people.

Ezekiel is in much better shape than he was at the end of the first chapter. There he was flat on his face before the Lord. Now he is standing tall before the Lord. There he was overwhelmed by his own inadequacy. Now he stands in the power of the Spirit the Lord has given to him. The same man, but another man and the Lord was the difference.

3

Briars, Thorns, and Assorted Scorpions

Ezekiel 2:3-8

It feels so good to get back on your feet after you've been flat on your face! The world doesn't look half so bad as it did when you were lying on it facedown. Just to get the dust out of your teeth and the sand out of your hair, brush down your clothes and empty your sandals makes all the difference in the world. You may even feel embarrassed that you let things get you down, but you soon forget about that because everything looks and feels so much better. Even Tel-abib doesn't look or smell so bad once you return with the new Spirit inside you! In fact, you might even get around to saying, "Boy, it's good to be alive."

Alive for what? Just to feel "up" till you get "down" again? To sink slowly in the west as regularly as the sun but not half so beautifully? Then to rise again with that awful sinking feeling always on the edge of your consciousness? To look continually for new ways of making the rising times more glorious and the sinking feelings less disastrous? To become wrapped up in methods and maneuvers designed to make your lot a happier one? One could get this impression by observing many Christians who have felt the Lord's gracious touch. But as Ezekiel was about to discover, God does not refresh and renew His people just so they can be as fresh and new as possible till the refreshing and renewing is once more necessary.

The intervention of God in the human experience is designed

to produce people who will be more readily equipped for His service. God stands people on their feet to send them on their way.

I Send Thee

The voice of the Lord broke in on Ezekiel's thoughts, "Son of man, I send thee to the children of Israel" (Ezek. 2:3). The words used by the Lord are remarkably similar to those spoken to Moses, Jeremiah, Isaiah, and Saul of Tarsus. The great statement of the Lord Jesus shortly before His ascension concerning the outpouring of the Holy Spirit made it clear that the Spirit would not come so they could have fun but that they might be empowered to be sent to Jerusalem, Judea, Samaria, and all parts of the world (Acts 1:8). This is clearly God's method of operation. He makes His people stand in the power of the Spirit and then sends them on their way in the enabling of the same Spirit.

Those who minister about the things of the Spirit and revel in such ministry have come under considerable attack from certain segments of the church. While the attack may sometimes be harsh, there are valid reasons for some of the criticism. There is little doubt that there are those who love to explore the intricacies of the "deeper life," the "exchanged life," the "victorious life," the "Spirit-filled life," and numerous other assorted "lives" without apparently finding it necessary to engage the "life" in any type of mission.

It is equally true that some of those who are deeply committed to the Church's mission have adopted some dangerous attitudes to ministries aimed at deepening the spiritual life of the believer. Some even seem to think that such ministry is unnecessary or a luxury that the crying needs of our contemporary world do not allow us to enjoy. God's word to Ezekiel shows us the correct balance.

As a boy I was introduced to the Keswick Convention in the English Lake District. (In fact, I understand I made my inauspicious debut there at the age of eight months!) The published purposes of the week-long meetings are to "promote practical holiness." But it is important to note that the great climax of the week is the meeting where world missions is emphasized and people are invited to demonstrate their commitment to the Lord Jesus by walking in Him in holiness of life and reaching those for whom Christ died.

One day I had the opportunity to preach at one of the Keswick missionary meetings. At the conclusion of the message a tall, dignified bishop came up to me and said, "Twenty-five years ago I stood in this tent to show my commitment to the Lord and that I was ready to be sent by Him anywhere at anytime. For over 20 years I have served Him in the Far East, but today my two children stood to give themselves to Him with the same commitment." I think Ezekiel would have understood the bishop's joy.

A Matter of Authority

When the Lord Jesus was busy about His Father's business, He met many skeptics. He loved to tell them that the Father had sent Him. Obviously, He felt this was something of great significance. The skeptics needed to understand that when they had dealings with the Son they were actually having dealings with the Father who had sent Him. They must accept the Son as they professed reverence for the Father, because the fact that He had been sent by the Father meant that the authority of the Father rested upon Him. He came in the Father's name.

We have three teenagers in our family and not enough bathrooms—no house has enough bathrooms for three teenagers! One day our youngest was hurling bloodcurdling threats through the bathroom door at his sister. He was having no discernible influence at all. In desperation, he came to me and delivered what to my masculine ear sounded like a perfectly valid complaint. I told him to stop threatening all manner of evil and simply say, "Dad sent me to tell you that it's time for us to leave for church and you must vacate the bathroom at once if not sooner." It worked! Not because our son had suddenly found favor in the eyes of his sister but because our daughter realized that she was being confronted with the awesome authority of Dad. "I was finished anyway," she said, as she swept past me into the car with a toss of her head and the slightest hint of a sheepish grin.

Ezekiel was about to discover that the Lord was going to bestow upon him the authority that comes from being sent on a mission by God. Moses had a similar experience as he was sent to confront Pharaoh (see Ex. 7—12). Gideon was told to go against the Midianites, even though he was reluctant almost to the point of insubordination. As he went, the Lord added the telling information that Gideon's strength lay in the fact that God had sent him (Jud. 6:11—7). Numerous other instances could be drawn from Scripture, but perhaps the most pertinent one for our purposes is found in some of the last words of the Lord. "All power (authority) is given unto Me. . . . Go ye therefore . . . and lo, I am with you" (Matt. 28:18-20).

Death to Apathy
Among Christians there is a strange reticence toward realistically challenging the world in which we live. Perhaps it comes from a sense of insecurity or inadequacy or possibly even apathy. I'm not sure how to handle apathy, but I do know that insecure people need to be convinced that the Lord Jesus said, "As My Father hath sent Me, even so send I you" (John 20:21) and that this commission is to be seen as the imparting of authority. To believe this is to be compelled to a whole new dimension of service.

I have been involved in many apparently ridiculous situations in my ministry, yet I have often continued in a situation only because I was convinced that the Lord had authorized me to be in that place at that time in that situation to be His representative. Often when I was tempted to throw in the towel and encouraged to quit by human considerations and perhaps even satanic suggestions, I pushed on solely because I was convinced that the One who had sent me there had not told me to move on. There comes a time when believers must stop backing off and start to speak and act with calm determination and a sense of unruffled authority. Provided, of course, that all concerned are quite clear that the authority is derived!

Romanticizing the Ministry
The sailors in the film *South Pacific* felt that they had been cheated. They had joined the Navy to see the world and what did they see? They saw the sea. They found that the Atlantic wasn't romantic, the Pacific wasn't terrific, and the Navy itself wasn't what it was cracked up to be.

Some people have been greatly excited about what they believed to be God's commission in their lives. They have thrown themselves with great enthusiasm and much sacrifice into Christian activities only to become desperately disillusioned and discouraged. They had been under the impression it would be romantic and terrific, only to find out it wasn't. Those who encouraged them to engage in the particular avenue of service were somewhat guilty of enhancing the situation and romanticizing the ministry to such an extent that the unsuspecting, bright-eyed candidate was led into sad disillusion.

No one could say the Lord painted rose-colored pictures for Ezekiel. Nothing but the plain, unvarnished truth came from the lips of the Lord to the startled ears of the son of man. "I send thee to a rebellious nation . . . they are impudent children and stiffhearted. I do send thee unto them" (2:3-4).

The Lord Jesus handled His disciples in similar fashion. "Behold, I send you forth as sheep in the midst of wolves" (Matt. 10:16). He hardly glamorized the role they were to play, and He did nothing to tone down the immensity of their task.

Impudence and Rebellion

The impudence and rebellion of which the Lord spoke had become the prevailing attitude of the people of God. They had a long, sad history of grumbling and rebelling. Ever since God had chosen to deal in a special way with Abraham and his descendants, they had been a problem people. But the Lord had stuck with them because He was committed to demonstrating to the surrounding nations the many facets of His nature and the glorious richness of His character. This was His basic purpose in calling them to Himself to be a "peculiar treasure" (Ex. 19:5). They were to be the model of how He dealt with people and He wanted them to relate to Him.

The people of God were aware of this great privilege and at times even bragged about it to their neighbors, but this did not deter them from grossly abusing it. Despite the fact that they knew the Lord had so identified Himself with them that to a certain extent His reputation was tied in with their behavior, they went ahead and misbehaved anyway. The Lord continually reminded them of their awesome responsibility and special privilege, but their rebellious, impudent attitude prevailed. But still He persisted. Spokesman followed spokesman; prophets, priests, and kings were anointed one after the other. The Lord spoke clearly, but still they rebelled.

It was into this environment that God planned to launch Ezekiel. Ezekiel must have known enough history to be aware that a prophet's life expectancy was not among the highest and that the fringe benefits of his new profession would be on the fringe!

Exercise in Futility

For God to continue to speak to those who refused to listen seems to be an exercise in futility, but God did not regard it as such. If people were to know Him in His fullness, it was necessary that they see Him in action in every situation. When the people of God went along with His principles, therefore, He released the unmistakable blessing that enriched His people in every dimension. But as the fount of all justice and the epitome of holiness, He finds it necessary to deal firmly and justly with sin. Accordingly, His people soon learned not only the blessing of God but the judgment of God. They were taught in first grade what they could expect from God when they obeyed or disobeyed Him.

God's grace and justice had been vividly demonstrated to the nations for hundreds of years through His dealings with His people. Perhaps the Hittites, the Amalekites, and all the other "ites" had been upset that God gave His people so much when they lived according to His principles, but they were most likely highly relieved not to be in a "special relationship" when judgment was being administered.

But that's how it is when you belong to the people of God. You are involved in God's revelation of Himself in all the wonders of His Being and that means blight and blessing, joy and judgment. God was telling Ezekiel that the people of Israel and the surrounding nations needed to be reminded of the reality of His Being. And Ezekiel was going to tell them whether they wanted to hear or not!

Thus Saith the Lord

The Lord quickly set the tone for Ezekiel's ministry. "Thou shalt say to them, 'Thus saith the Lord' " (2:4).

With time on their hands, the people of the exile probably spent long hours discussing and debating. They had no football scores to discuss, no batting averages to memorize. There was no television show to relive, and no one was running for office. Inflation was not a factor. In fact, there was little to talk about but their present situation, its causes and solutions. The bitter blamed the politicians, some blamed themselves, others blamed God. The romantics dreamed of the good old days, the firebrands dreamed of revolt. The visionaries plotted dramatic mass escapes, and the pragmatists figured that if they couldn't beat the system, they might as well join it. There were as many ideas as people and as many solutions as ideas. But they were all limited to the people's understanding of the dilemma.

One opinion was not often voiced and on the rare occasions it was voiced, it was summarily dismissed. The one who had voiced it was also dismissed! Nevertheless, it was the opinion that alone was worth hearing—the opinion of the Lord. Surely He would know why they were where they were, how long they would be there, what to do while they were there and how they were going to get out and when! He did know and He would tell, but the people didn't want to hear.

God wanted them to know. He told Ezekiel to avoid any speculation about the situation, join the debates, and say, "Gentlemen, there is one opinion that is accurate and one opinion only that is really worth hearing, and I am ready to give it to you. Are you ready? 'Thus saith the Lord. . . .' "

Thorns and Briars

The Lord told Ezekiel what to expect, as was His custom when sending His servants. He told Ezekiel the way the people would look at him, the things they would say to him, and the actions they would take against him. Their faces would be hard, their gaze unflinching, their demeanor unyielding, their attitude unrelenting (2:6). Their words would be harsh and bitter, their manner caustic, their attacks vicious. It would be like someone running through briars and thorns, being ripped to shreds, and falling exhausted to the ground bleeding and hurting, only to land on a scorpion and be stung.

Ezekiel could anticipate being bitten and ripped, abused and rejected, but he was to go anyway. God's truth must be released and God's people must be exposed to their own condition. God had to do it to be consistent with His own nature. He had to do it to be faithful to His own people. He had to deal with His people so that the nations around would know the truth of God.

Don't Chicken Out

God's dealing with Ezekiel at this point seem to be almost merciless, but two things should not be overlooked. The Lord showed how thoroughly He understands human nature in general and Ezekiel in particular.

In a situation like the one just described, He knew that human beings tend to do one of two things. Rather than go against the stream and engage in head-to-head conflict concerning the things of God, we either chicken out on the assignment or join the opposition. We take a good long look at our world and see the necessity to confront it in the name of the Lord, yet we tend to say, "It's hopeless, it's dangerous, I'm going home." Or, "Nothing I can do will ever change this. They don't want to be changed; the whole idea is ridiculous. I can't beat the situation, I'll just join it."

Notice the two specific instructions the Lord gave Ezekiel: Don't be like they are; don't be afraid to speak (2:8).

Let's Evaluate Ezekiel

I wonder how the contemporary church would have rated Ezekiel. It all depends on the criteria used to evaluate his ministry. Often the situation in which we find ourselves determines the standards we use. When I first became interested in the work of the Church in England, I heard an old-timer from a small struggling fellowship say with great feeling, "God doesn't want us to be successful. He just expects us to be faithful." Immediately one of his friends jumped up and added, "Amen. We aren't interested in anything spectacular. We only want things to be scriptural."

But in the U.S., where planning, organizing, and evaluating is a major part of the national genius, the church plans, organizes, and evaluates and tends to measure success and effectiveness by statistics. When a pastor's work is being considered, the following questions are often asked:

1. What is the annual budget of your church?
2. What was the budget when you began your pastorate?
3. What is the Sunday morning attendance?
4. What was the attendance when you started your ministry?
5. What percentage of your budget is devoted to world missions?
6. What was the percentage when you arrived at the church?
7. What is the church's indebtedness?
8. What was the indebtedness when you accepted your call?

Many factors other than the ones mentioned above need to be borne in mind when evaluating a ministry because these criteria are inadequate in themselves. For instance, in the U.S. it is still considered respectable to maintain membership in a church and to attend with some degree of regularity, but in England the population has failed to see the importance of church attendance since the end of World War II. So in the U.S. one can count church members, but in England the ministry may not be as readily measurable. In fact, it may be that a ministry in England which produces 50 disciples is considerably more effective than a ministry in America which produces 500.

Who Pays for the Heating?

The U.S. government graciously allows a tax break to those who give to the church of their choice, but in England the government sees no necessity to help pay the church heating bills or the support of missionaries. This would lead us to anticipate that giving per church member in the U.S. would be greater than giving per church member in other parts of the world. If this is true, it can be at least partially attributed to the aid of the government. Giving, therefore, may not be the greatest or the most accurate means of measuring spiritual effectiveness.

The church attendance on Sunday and Wednesday evenings has long been a standard of evaluation. Someone has even gone so far as to say, "The attendance on Sunday morning shows the popularity of the church, on Sunday evening the popularity of the preacher, and on Wednesday, the popularity of the Lord Jesus." But in all fairness it should be pointed out that people are more likely to attend a service on the beach in California when the temperature is in the 80s than to go to a service in downtown Detroit, where they may get mugged. And more people will attend a Wednesday evening service if they live in an area where little is going on and they are simply waiting for something to happen than in a suburb where the men and women commute to work.

It would seem, then, that we should not use any kind of evaluation, but to arrive at this conclusion would be a mistake. On the Day of Pentecost someone took the trouble to estimate the number of those who were brought into a relationship with the Lord Jesus, and the Holy Spirit gave the "go ahead" for the information to be recorded (Acts 2:41). We know how many people the Lord fed on the mountainside (John 6:10), how much water He turned into wine at the wedding at Cana (John 2:6), and the amount of one woman's offering (Luke 21:2).

A Prophet among Them

As I see it, there is only one safe way to evaluate a ministry and that is to interpret it in the light of the objective of God for that ministry, considering the circumstances under which the ministry was established. The Lord did not give any scale of evaluation to Ezekiel but He did tell him what to expect and what to do. Even though the Lord knew the work would be hard, the people resistant, and the response small, He told Ezekiel to say to them, "Thus saith the Lord," and added, "Thou shalt speak My words to them" (Ezek. 2:7).

If Ezekiel wanted to know how he was doing, he did not need to worry about attendance, decision cards, budgets, or mortgages. All he had to do was check if he had really let the people know what the Lord was saying. The big question on his evaluation sheet was, "To what extent are the people becoming increasingly aware that God has spoken?" In fact, the Lord said that the people should "know that there had been a prophet among them" (2:5). Not a speaker popular in the business sector and warmly welcomed in the political and entertainment world, but a prophet from the Lord. Someone who had unflinchingly reminded the people that the Lord was still the Lord.

Instant Success

Prompt response is something important to the modern church. When we preach, we often want to see immediate results. But in Ezekiel's case, the results could not be seen quickly because the very nature of a prophet's ministry demands that some time elapse before its effect can be seen. The ministry of a prophet is authenticated only when the events he spoke about actually take place.

Ezekiel's task was unbelievably difficult. Not only did he have to go to a rebellious people with an unpopular message, knowing that they had a long history of rejecting, but he knew there was no way he could be accepted or his ministry authenticated for a considerable time. Ezekiel would rate rather poorly in today's church, but in God's Book he was great.

Leaving Results to Him

The more I study the ways of God in His dealings with mankind, the more I'm amazed.

When He told Jonah to go to Nineveh, the prophet immediately took off in the opposite direction. The Lord pursued him in an underwater vehicle, arranged for him to be unceremoniously received on board, taken to land, and coughed up safe if not very sound. Then, after all that trouble, He let him continue his ministry and actually see a phenomenal response. Even then Jonah was most uncooperative, but the Lord persisted.

Ezekiel was to see no such revival, however, or experience no such care. Neither was he going to engage in any kind of rebellious attitude or undertake any rebellious action. In fact, the Lord warned him not even to try anything like rebellion.

The Lord seemed remarkably lenient with Jonah and tough with Ezekiel. He let Jonah see much blessing and Ezekiel very little. All this ought to confirm that the important thing for every servant of God is to ensure that whatever means of evaluation are legitimate, nothing replaces the necessity for glad submission and instant obedience to Him and ongoing dependence on Him. The servant who does these things can work with joy and fervor and gratefully leave the results to Him, knowing full well that God's ways are not our ways.

4

The Woe Roll

Ezekiel 2:9—3

A hand appeared out of nowhere. No wrist, arm, or shoulder. Just a hand holding a roll or a scroll (Ezek. 2:9). It was not unlike the part of a man's hand that suddenly appeared at the wild party thrown by Belshazzar except that that hand only had fingers and the fingers wrote on the wall (Dan. 5:5). There is something unnerving about armless hands that appear holding scrolls or handless fingers that write on walls.

The hand slowly unrolled the scroll. Then Ezekiel noticed something odd about the scroll. Scrolls usually contained writing on only one side; this scroll had writing on both sides. "It was written within and without" is how the Bible explains it (2:10).

For years Bible scholars have been having a wonderful time trying to explain why the scroll had writing on both sides, like the one that John saw in his vision on the Isle of Patmos. One commentator from a bygone era believed that the writing on the "without" side had a literal meaning and the writing on the "within" held a mystical significance. More recent writers suggest that it probably meant the Lord had filled both sides of the scroll so that Ezekiel couldn't add anything on his own. I'm certain there is truth in both concepts, but perhaps the significance goes no deeper than the fact that the Lord had a lot to say to Ezekiel and needed both sides of the scroll to get it said. Rather like writing on every available inch of an aerogram.

Bad, Bad News

Ezekiel started to read; it was unpleasant reading. All the scroll contained were "lamentations, mournings, and woe" (2:10). Just bad, bad news.

God sometimes required prophets to go to the people and pronounce "woe" to them. They stood before the people as His agents and warned them that they were heading for trouble if they persisted in the way they were going. It was a kind of warning ministry. Obviously, it was not the most popular kind of ministry, and quite often the people told the prophet in no uncertain terms that they didn't want to hear what he had to say.

Nevertheless, the Lord continued in His "woe" ministries even through the work of the Lord Jesus, who did His own fair share of "woe-ing." "Woe unto you, scribes and Pharisees, hypocrites . . . ," He said many times (Matt. 23:13-29, Luke 11:44). "Woe to you, Chorazin, woe to you, Bethsaida . . . ," He proclaimed to two particularly unrepentant cities (Matt. 11:21).

The idea of the "woe" ministry was of course that the people being "woe-d" would heed the warning and repent. In a strange sort of way, this most unpopular style of ministry is one of the most gracious ministries to which God calls His people. What could be more thoughtful or more gracious than for God to give ample warning of what He is planning to do?

Puppet On a String

One of God's rules of operation is: warning before judgment. He has always been committed to the principle of clearly explaining to people that their actions have repercussions and that if the actions are out of order judgment will result.

He told Adam and Eve how He intended to carry on. They could not possibly have misunderstood God when He explained about the tree of the knowledge of good and evil. If they chose to eat of its fruit, they would face death. "Woe to you if you eat that fruit" would be another way of expressing what God said to them (Gen. 2:16-17). There was more fruit than they could possibly eat and more variety than they could ever desire, but God had to give them a choice or there would have been no point in giving them free wills.

Man without freedom of choice is a puppet on a string, and puppets can't love, serve, and glorify God. Options, therefore, are essential if man and God are to enjoy the relationship of mutual love and trust that God had in mind for the God-man relationship. Of course, God need only have made the options and not bothered to explain the ramifications of the choices offered. But He graciously and carefully explained that life would be enjoyed through obedience, and trouble would come from disobedience.

God in Mourning

The New Testament writer James nailed it down more precisely. He explained the whole thing from temptation through enticement leading to lust which becomes sin which inevitably leads to death (James 1:13-16). What he said was, in effect, "Woe to you if you insist on playing with temptation and putting yourself in the way of enticement, because sooner or later you will fall into sin and that leads to death."

It should be absolutely clear that God places great importance on the "woe" ministry even if His servants don't appreciate doing it and the people don't want to hear it. When woe ministries are ignored, the result is "lamentations and mourning." God cannot be ignored with impunity and His principles cannot be abused without disaster. But as human beings so often think they know better than God or hope they can get away with disobeying God, our society is wracked by pain and anguish which we could have been spared if the warnings had been heeded.

I believe it is legitimate for us to understand that not all the lamentations and the mourning are related to mankind. God mourns over His willful people. He laments the necessity of judgment. His loving heart yearns for the sinner and longs for the erring one to realize the folly of his way and return to the God who will abundantly pardon. Lovingly He kept sending His prophets, reminding His people, exposing their sins, refreshing their memories. With deep sorrow He spoke, with deep mourning He yearned.

Perhaps the most graphic demonstration of God's mourning for His creation and lamenting over the judgment that must fall on the unrepentant is Jesus' concern about Jerusalem. The city had repeatedly heard from the prophets through the years and from the Lord Jesus Himself that God must intervene if they refused to turn to Him. Like a hen sensing danger and instinctively rushing to gather her chickens under her wings, the Lord had tried to bring them to Himself. But they would not be brought (Matt. 23:37).

Pills and Rolls

The subject of judgment is least distressing when kept at a respectable distance. The mighty hand of God can get a little too close for comfort and the woe on the roll written within and without is more easily handled if it doesn't have to be handled. But God wanted Ezekiel to do more than handle the roll. He wanted him to eat it! I have thought of many responses to the command, "Eat this roll" (Ezek. 3:1).

"Thanks, but I've already eaten!"

"Sorry, I'm on a diet and I've given up rolls."

"I can't stand rolls. Particularly woe rolls."

But the response to such excuses would have been the same: "Eat this roll."

Our family pet is a particularly amiable Golden Retriever. One day our friend the vet told us Prince had a bad case of heart worm and his only chance of recovery was to take a very stiff course of pills. He showed us how to push the pill down the dog's throat despite his gagging and choking. We thought the cure was worse than the disease, so we tried to find gentler ways of giving our pet his medicine. We hid it in his dish of food. He ate the food, carefully left the pill right in the middle of the dish, and then scrupulously licked all round it. Not to be outdone, we gave him one of his favorite candies with the pill carefully hidden inside. He gratefully swallowed the candy and gently laid the pill on the floor. We tried cake next. The cake was promptly gobbled, but the pill remained. By this time he realized we were introducing him to a new game called Find the Pill. He loved it and won every round. Finally we admitted defeat, bowed to the superior wisdom of our friend the veterinarian, and learned all over again that when bitter things have to be swallowed, the only way is to swallow them.

Thou Shalt Not Nibble

The Lord made it quite clear to Ezekiel that He intended the roll to be completely eaten. Not nibbled like a frothy dessert or avoided like something hazardous to health, but eaten with or without enthusiasm.

When it comes to feeding on the Word, people tend to agree

with the Lord that they cannot live by bread alone. But then they try to show how much living they can do on as little word from the Lord as possible. They diet the heavy things of God out of their menu. They avoid the nutritious things that need chewing, and whenever they come across something that makes them gag, they treat it with selective rejection, laying it delicately on the edge of their plates.

When Ezekiel saw the Lord's intention, he opened his mouth and began to eat. Or nibble like a missionary being introduced to monkey meat. "Son of man, cause thy belly to eat, and fill thy bowels with this roll that I give thee" (Ezek. 3:3) was the instruction. The references to such indelicate subjects as "belly" and "bowels" may seem out of place in our civilized society even if they are attributed to the Almighty! The Lord was impressing upon Ezekiel that He would no more tolerate half-hearted nibbling on the truth than He would accept selective rejection of it. He wanted Ezekiel to feed so thoroughly on the roll that it would be completely digested and find its way into the bloodstream of his life and the fiber of his being.

The assimilation of the Word needs to be strongly emphasized in this day and age. Digesting food so thoroughly that it is assimilated by the body and being of a person requires time and the balanced function of a healthy body. So it is with the Word the Lord has for His people. Time taken to read it, mark it, learn it, and inwardly digest it is time that needs to be as carefully planned into the daily life-style of the believer as time for work and rest. But it is a rare thing to find this happening in the lives of God's frenetic people.

It is ironic that Eastern cults are moving into our frantic society preaching the gospel of meditation. The particular brand of meditation being advocated must be rejected because of its dangerous connotations and implications, but the necessity for quiet contemplation and meditation is something the believer must advocate. Strange as it may seem, there is a sad shortage of Christians who believe in taking time to obey the command of Scripture, "Meditate upon these things" (1 Tim. 4:15), while unbelievers with nothing more than their navels to contemplate go ahead and contemplate anyway.

If food is to be adequately handled by the body, it must be eaten in manageable pieces. The same is true with the truth of

God, which is to be the staple diet of the believer. This requires the developing of skills to rightly handle and correctly divide the Word of God. I am constantly alarmed by the glib approach of those who profess to believe the Bible from "cover to cover." Many appear to have little more than a nodding acquaintance with anything between the covers.

But even when time is planned for quiet study and methods are devised for rightly dividing the Word of God, it is still necessary that material being taken in is digested by the correct juices. It takes more than study techniques and organization of time to get the food into the system. Faith in what God reveals is one of the juices, and obedience to what God requires is the other. When the believer carefully regulates his intake of truth and assiduously trusts and obeys what the truth puts into him, then the miracle of digestion takes place and the food changes from being a lump in the mouth to strength in the muscles, blood in the veins, and energy in the brain. To be motivated and strengthened daily by the truth assimilated is one of the basic requirements for normal spiritual health.

How Sweet It Is

Paul expressed similar sentiments when he encouraged the Colossians to "Let the Word of Christ dwell in you richly" (Col. 3:16). Both the Colossian believers and Ezekiel needed to heed the word of God about the Word of God. For Ezekiel, it was far from easy. Remember, it was a woe roll he was handed by a hand that appeared from nowhere! Ezekiel had to allow the awesome truth of God to sink into his innermost being. God was giving him solemn warnings on which to feed. The promises he received were promises of divine intervention in the affairs of the people of God that would have harmful repercussions.

He began to allow God's solemn truth and dire predictions to become the fire of his bones and the motivating factor in his life. His will was nerved by something other than attractive promises, and his mind was fed by a divinely prescribed diet of apparently unpalatable truth. And another strange thing happened. The bitter roll became "as honey for sweetness" (Ezek. 3:3).

I hated spinach when I was a kid. My brother loathed tomatoes. To our mother these facts were at best incidental and at worst irrelevant. When it came to matters of diet, her approach was a model of simplicity: "Eat what you're given!" Many a confrontation at the meal table ended with a firm look and determined statement, "It's for your own good." As we were given no options, my brother and I ate what we were given. As the years went by something most peculiar happened. I became a spinacholic and my brother needs treatment for his tomatoholism.

Over the years, I have had problems with some aspects of God's truth. The wrath of God, election, separation, the Church, and elders have all been unpalatable in varying degrees at some time in my spiritual feeding. But I have learned one thing about unpalatable truth—eat it anyway, because it's for my own good. I do not want to give the impression that I have arrived at such a pinnacle of spirituality that I can now digest all doctrines without any trace of spiritual indigestion. I once heard John R. W. Stott answer a difficult question with the words, "I feel that is one area in which it is necessary to exercise some reverent agnosticism." Nevertheless, even though I still choke and cough, gag and splutter at times, I have found the Word of God inexpressibly sweet even in some of its toughest pronouncements. The tougher statements of Scripture often burn hotter in my bones than some of the gentler utterances.

To believe God in the hard sayings and to trust the Lord in the difficult things is indescribably sweet. In very truth, "Tis so sweet to trust in Jesus."

Do It

As the bittersweet roll disappeared into the prophet Ezekiel and the sweetness of God's truth began to energize his being, the Lord pressed home the significance of the vision. "Son of man, go, get thee unto the house of Israel and speak My words unto them (Ezek. 3:4). There was nothing new about these instructions, but evidently in God's opinion, Ezekiel didn't need anything new. He needed to get on with the truth he already knew!

I freely admit some uneasiness about this idea, because something in me enjoys digging out new truth more than doing what I already know. I am much more comfortable in searching the Word of God for more information than in putting into operation the latest piece of truth received from the Lord. I think my situation is not particularly unique. Naturally, having to do what you know is much more challenging than simply attending a seminar to learn how to do what you probably have little intention of doing.

Perhaps I am overly critical, but I suspect that the Church may be catering to people's reluctance to do things by putting on innumerable seminars and training sessions to teach them how to do them. By the time the people have attended all the seminars, they can legitimately say that they don't have the time to do anything about the things they learned in the seminar. And by the time they have explained that point, it's time to go to the next seminar!

Knowing what to do is of little value unless it is coupled with doing what you know. Ezekiel had received enough vision to get him headed in the right direction. But when you remember the direction in which he was required to head, perhaps we can understand why he may have preferred a little more vision to moving into action. Perhaps he thought, "I do like a good vision. Nothing inspires me more. The grandeur and the color, the mystery and the excitement are superb. And to be reminded of God's transcendence and immanence in such graphic ways is something I will never forget. And I adore sweet rolls. But I am a little apprehensive about all those hard-faced, tough-minded, God-ignoring fellow travelers of mine. So, Lord, how about an instant replay of the vision. Preferably in slow motion!" But the Lord was not about to get into that kind of thing. "Go, get thee to the house of Israel."

Some reminders about hard faces, strong foreheads, rebellious looks, and bad attitudes followed, and then the Lord said, "Behold, I have made thy face strong against their faces and thy forehead strong against their foreheads" (3:8). God was telling Ezekiel that a lot of head butting was about to begin, but he shouldn't worry about that because he had been equipped with a strong head. A small point perhaps, but a great reminder of God's attention to details when it comes to the preparing of His people for testimony and ministry.

After the Vision

To the accompaniment of the now familiar sounds of the whirring wheels and whirling wings, Ezekiel sensed that he was being taken up by the Spirit and he found himself back in the familiar surroundings of Tel-abib (3:12-15).

We have no way of knowing how long he had been absent. It is possible that the vision, like a dream, was over in seconds. It is also conceivable that he had wandered in the desert for days, lost in his experience of God. Perhaps his wife had searched for him frantically or maybe he had lain like a log in full view of the exiles but they, sensing the mystery of what was transpiring in their fellow camper, had simply stood and watched. We don't know *how* everything happened, but we are told *what* happened when he returned to Tel-abib. We know exactly what he did. He did nothing. Absolutely nothing! For seven days he just sat where the people sat. He said nothing; he just sat and stared.

Outwardly nothing was going on, but inside the prophet was seething. The King James Version says he was "astonished" (3:15) but the word is better translated in stronger terms. The same word is used to describe a bear's response to losing her cubs. The men who joined David in the cave of Adullam (1 Sam. 22:1-2) were more than astonished, they were thoroughly disgruntled and mad about things. It is more accurate to say that while Ezekiel sat in splendid silence among the exiles, he was thoroughly angry and deeply perturbed.

We are not sure what was making him so angry. Some think he was angry that God had put him in such an invidious situation. "Why did God pull me out from the crowd and give me the job of being spokesman? I didn't ask for the job, and life is frustrating enough without being stuck with this kind of responsibility."

Others believe it is more likely that after his great experience with the Lord, Ezekiel would hardly be angry *with* God but would more likely be angry *for* God. He had tasted the sweetness of God's dealings with His people. The "lamentations, mourning, and woe" had shown him the heart of a mourning, just God who had to pronounce "woe" but whose mercy insisted in warning repeatedly and persistently that the judgment must fall. This seems to be closer to the true meaning of the emotional reaction of Ezekiel. Like the Lord Jesus in the temple centuries later, he looked at the God-rejecting people with anger and felt consumed with the "zeal of the Lord." A man in this frame of mind can do some silly things, but Ezekiel was in good hands. In fact, "the hand of the Lord was strong upon me" was how he explained God's reassuring, restraining hand (3:14).

God's Gift to Tel-abib
People who sit among their friends for seven days without saying

a word are usually regarded as being just a little strange. Ezekiel was no exception. What was going on in his tortured mind no one knows except the Lord. For seven days the Lord left His man free to sit and stare. But when He thought it was time to move, the word of the Lord came again to Ezekiel. Prefaced by the familiar, "son of man," the Lord announced that He had "given" Ezekiel as a watchman to the house of Israel (3:17). Note the word "given" which is not in some translations of the Bible. It highlights an important truth. It reminds us that the Lord regarded Ezekiel not only as His servant but also as His own special gift to the house of Israel. God alone knew how desperately the people in exile needed a watchman. They didn't seem to realize their need, but the Lord did and He acted. This action once again shows that God, even in times of national disgrace and disintegration, cares for the people amongst whom He is working. Even when the people of the land ignore Him and resent Him, He still brings gifts even though they may well be refused and abused.

Judgment to some degree had already fallen on the rebellious people. Their exile was a daily reminder of this, but God had graciously permitted the judgment to come in installments, hoping that repentance and restoration would result. Mercifully He withheld much of the judgment so richly deserved. Jerusalem was not completely denuded of His people. There were still evidences of His presence in the rebellious city, but more judgment was slated if the people didn't repent. A watchman was needed for the interim, and God provided one for His people.

The Watchman

Every city had its watchman in Ezekiel's day. The walled cities in which the people lived for safety had gates through which the traffic passed. Each evening the gates were closed and the watchman's lonely, cold vigil began. His job was to scan the horizon, keeping his eyes peeled for anything that might spell danger to the city. He could see much farther than the people in the streets because of his elevated position and because he was not involved in the common distractions of everyday living. If he saw something important, he announced it to the people of the city, and thus alerted them to the possible need to defend the city. Wise people deeply appreciated good watchmen.

Ezekiel's role was quite clear. God had said, "I have made thee a watchman unto the house of Israel" (3:17). He had a special view of the spiritual horizon because of his special relationship with the Lord. His elevated position and devoted attention gave him a unique opportunity to see impending doom and to warn the people in time for them to take action. The Lord wanted the people to have all the warning He could provide for them, but He couldn't make them believe or even listen.

Watchmen are not always popular. Sometimes they are deeply resented. When Winston Churchill insisted on telling the British Parliament in the late 1930s that Hitler was rearming Germany, they ostracized him. They didn't want to know. The more he told them Hitler was not to be trusted the more they decided it was Churchill who shouldn't be trusted. But he was right. After the war he again became watchman to the free world. "Stalin is a rogue and is on the make," became his theme. Once again he was maligned, and once again he was right. Aleksandr Solzhenitzyn may be in the same category. Only time will tell, though we don't need time to tell us that large segments of American society deeply resent this man who keeps stirring up people's fears about the Soviet Union. Being a watchman to people who don't want to be warned can be a lonely, cold existence.

The Wicked and the Righteous

The Lord told Ezekiel that he would have to give warnings to two categories of people: the "wicked" and the "righteous." To the wicked he was to announce, "If you continue in your wickedness you will die in your sin" (3:18). To the righteous he was to say, "If you turn from your righteousness and commit iniquity you shall die in your sin" (3:20).

Ezekiel was then warned that he might fail in his task and if he didn't give the people God's message, he would be partly responsible for the death of both the wicked and the righteous— God said He would require the blood of these people "at thine hand" (3:20). He added that if Ezekiel told the people and they refused to respond, Ezekiel would not be held responsible (3:21).

These words must have been nerve-wracking to Ezekiel, and many Christians' nerves have been wracked by them as well.

There is something of a problem for Christians in the statement that the righteous will suffer the same fate as the wicked if they revert to sinful ways. The problem is caused by Christians assuming that Old Testament righteousness is synonymous with New Testament justification. This confusion leads us to the enormous error that the justified can lose their justification if they sin.

In Old Testament times, some people genuinely endeavored to fulfill the commandments of God and to carefully adhere to the conditions laid down by Jehovah for a meaningful relationship with Him on the basis of the Covenant made to Abraham. They were the righteous. However, no one was ever brought to the position of justification through this kind of righteousness, because as Scripture states clearly, "by the works of the law shall no flesh be justified" (Gal. 2:16). In the Old Testament times as well as New Testament times people came to the position of being justified by faith. Abraham is clearly shown as one who experienced justification by faith and not by his adherence to any system of righteous works.

What Ezekiel was told to say, in effect, was, "You folks who care nothing for God need to know that if you persist in your disregard of God, you will die as a sinner. Those of you who are religious and earnest about trying to live the good life need to know the same thing. One of these days, you will trip up in your efforts and realize you are just as capable of sinning as the wicked. Therefore, both of you need to know that you are in danger of divine judgment unless you come in repentance and faith to God."

Blood on Our Hands

Then there is the problem of "blood on our hands." This sounds gruesome to our delicate ears but is perhaps best understood in terms of the principle that God taught Noah. "Whoso sheds man's blood, by man shall his blood be shed" (Gen. 9:6). The idea is that a watchman who knows the truth about a person's spiritual danger and fails to alert him is some kind of spiritual murderer. How far this can be applied to a Christian without driving him to a nervous breakdown is not clear. Obviously, the Christian cannot warn everybody, but he has the responsibility of warning someone.

Perhaps what we all need to realize is the immense importance the Lord attaches to sharing what you know with those who don't know. Surely this will lead all earnest children of God to a responsible life of ministry and deliver them from a life of careless, callous indifference.

After imparting this chilling information to Ezekiel, the Lord led him back to the plains where he saw a rerun of the vision that had started the whole experience. And then a strange and weird thing happened again—the Lord told Ezekiel to go and shut himself up in his house. Can you believe that? Well, then, you'll be ready for the next bombshell. God said, "Thou shalt be dumb" (Ezek. 3:26). For good measure, Ezekiel would also have some kind of restraints put on him (3:25). We are not sure exactly what this means. Some think that the people of Tel-abib decided to "lock him up" because of his strange behavior. Others think that he was placed under some kind of house arrest because the people resented him so much.

We don't know, but we do know this. God moves in mysterious ways His wonders to perform. Some people hear that and say, "You've got to be kidding. You don't really believe that God is so crazy, do you? Forget about God and put it all down to cruel fate." Reverent hearts however, keep trusting, and say with the Apostle Paul, "O the depth of the riches both of the wisdom and knowledge of God! How unsearchable are His judgments, and His ways past finding out!" (Rom. 11:33)

5

How Odd of God!

Ezekiel 4—7

Some incidents make unbelievers out of people. God had told Ezekiel, "Thou shalt speak My words to them" (3:4). Then He said, "I will make thy tongue cleave to the roof of thy mouth that thou shalt be dumb" (3:26). From a purely rational point of view, unbelief or skepticism is understandable. Many people think if God is really calling a man to speak for Him He would surely not strike him dumb! Therefore, if the man senses a call and then loses his voice, it is reasonable to assure that either he was wrong about the call or he became the unfortunate victim of unavoidable circumstances which God could not or would not change. To think like this, however, is to leave out one strange possibility, namely, that God sometimes chooses to work in ways that appear totally irrational to earth people.

Scripture repeatedly tells us that there is method in what appears to be God's madness. The Lord had His excellent reasons for calling Ezekiel to speak and then taking away his speaking equipment. Paul explained to the Corinthians that God chooses weak things to defeat strong things, foolish things to confuse wise things, things that are disregarded to overcome the highly regarded so that "no flesh should glory in His presence" (1 Cor. 1:27-29).

Suppose God had gone about things the way we would go about them. He would have given Ezekiel lessons in speech, classes in rhetoric, groomed his television image, and promoted his good looks. The result probably would have been crowds flocking to hear the polished, well-groomed, articulate presentations of a highly talented, thoroughly trained man.

God knows the dangers of our kind of approach even if the contemporary church doesn't. Therefore, He has a delightful way of confounding the critics by raising up someone to be His agent who is so handicapped that even the most skeptical person has to admit that this person's effectiveness depends on something bigger than his handicap and greater than his ability. The skeptic may even get around to calling this "greater thing" God and perhaps even glorify Him. Whether he does or not is of secondary importance, because God has given ample evidence to recognize that "the excellency of the power [is] of God and not of us" (2 Cor. 4:7). This kind of situation can be tough on the man who wants to serve God, but he soon learns that serving the living and true God is not for sissies. When the Lord's people get around to serving Him for His glory, they learn quickly that it is the Lord who matters and it is they who are expendable.

Some of Paul's most fruitful work was done while he was in prison and possibly because he was imprisoned. The most exciting missionary development of the Early Church was the result of persecution (Acts 8:1-4). The basis of all God's work in behalf of a fallen humanity was a cross.

There is some doubt about the exact nature of Ezekiel's dumbness. We know that the Lord gave it to him and also promised to release him from it at certain times. We also know that the dumbness was finally terminated when news of the fall of Jerusalem reached Tel-abib. Some people think Ezekiel's problem was not a literal dumbness but a ceremonial dumbness in which Ezekiel obeyed the Lord's command not to speak anything other than the words the Lord gave him. Others are of the opinion that it was a real, physical malady that the Lord overcame miraculously whenever He had something to say through His servant. Either way, the results were the same. God spoke through a man who was so severely handicapped that it was obvious God was the source of both his message and his strength.

Ezekiel on TV?

God's flexibility and creative genius are also clearly demonstrated in the way He led and used Ezekiel. He instructed the "son of man" to do all kinds of dramatic things even though he could not say anything particularly gripping.

Here's a lesson for the Church. God has innumerable creative ideas and a multitude of initiatives He can take to get across the full, dramatic force of His truth. But, unfortunately, His Church is not always enthusiastic about being creative and is considerably less than avant garde when it comes to communication. For instance, some people have seen the possibilities of using the mass media to communicate God's truth, but most of them use the camera to eavesdrop on a service designed for those who are present rather than for those who are sitting at home. Surely something dramatic and creative is called for if we are ever to successfully use the mass media!

Ezekiel would have been a natural on TV. Imagine how he would have gripped the people's attention in no time at all. Think how he would have portrayed such striking images that the watchers would never have forgotten either the message he brought or the truth he conveyed.

But he had no mass media and no vast crowds. Just a dusty house in a drab settlement populated by disgruntled people.

The Mud Brick

One day, at the Lord's instructions, Ezekiel appeared outside his front door with a large mud brick (4:1). He started to draw a scene on it. A crowd quickly gathered round—people always want to see what someone is drawing or painting.

"Looks like the Jerusalem skyline to me."

"Right, there's the temple."

"What are you doing, Ezekiel? Trying to earn a buck doing sidewalk art?"

"What's the point of all this, man? Why don't you say something?"

Silence reigned except for the scratching of a tool on brick. Suddenly, Ezekiel stopped his drawing, put the brick down in the sand, squatted on his haunches, and silently began to build sand forts (4:2). The crowd loved it till they saw that he was building a model of Jerusalem surrounded by military encampments and mounds of earth level with the city walls so that archers could shoot over the walls. The meaning was clear. He was telling the people that Jerusalem's troubles were far from over—the worst was yet to come! He shuffled into his lowly little house and came out carrying the flat iron pan that he used for baking bread over the fire (4:3).

"Time for supper, Ezekiel?"

"Can we all stay for some of your fresh baked bread?"

Silence. He put the plate down between him and the model of the surrounded city.

"What do you mean by all this, Ezekiel?"

"Is this what you were dreaming about the last seven days?"

"D'you think he's trying to tell us that an iron curtain has descended between the Lord and the city and that it will soon be overthrown?"

Still Ezekiel said nothing, but lying down on his left side, he watched the model of Jerusalem, apparently oblivious to the crowd around him (4:4).

Ezekiel became something of an institution. Day after day the people came by to see what was going on at his house. For weeks and months nothing much happened. In fact, for 390 days he could be seen lying beside his model of the besieged city. He had even taken to wearing ropes and chains (4:8).

One day somebody shouted, "Hey, Ezekiel has turned over onto his right side!"

But that was all that happened for another 40 days. There is no way of knowing what the reactions of the people were, but Ezekiel's message was quite simple. The Lord was predicting the fall of Jerusalem, the withdrawal of His presence there, and that things were going to be desperate for a long, long time.

Each day that Ezekiel lay on his side represented a year. The "years" spent on his left side represented the time of Israel's troubles, while the time on his right side symbolized the length of Judah's punishment. If you are mathematically inclined, you may want to count the days and see how it all fits in with the time schedule recorded in the prophecy. If you do work it all out, you will find that Ezekiel had no time to spare.

Bread and Water

While he was acting out his dramatic presentation, Ezekiel was eating starvation rations. The Lord limited him to a daily diet of about eight ounces bread and about one pint of water (4:9-11).

The Scriptures do not indicate that Ezekiel lay outside his

house all day every day for over a year or that the bread and
water diet was all he had to eat. It is quite possible that he spent
part of the time outside eating his symbolic meal and lying on
his symbolic and sore side, then was free to eat and sleep in the
privacy of his home, but this is not necessarily the case.

When the Lord told him to cook the bread over a fire using
human excrement as fuel, Ezekiel strongly objected. As a candidate for the priesthood, he had meticulously observed the rules on
food and ceremonial purity, and to cook his food that way was
unthinkable. The Lord immediately lowered the requirements to
animal dung, but it would appear the point being made was that
the fallen city would suffer terrible starvation and all manner of
human indignities (4:12-15).

What a Way to Shave

The crowd got excited one day when Ezekiel moved into a different activity after his long, strange inactivity. He got hold of a
sword (correct translation of "knife") which he sharpened on one
side so that it was as keen as a razor (5:1). Given his peculiar
behavior to date, his audience was probably unenthusiastic about
sitting on the front rows, just in case he got too "happy" with his
sword! Suddenly he began to shave his beard and chop off his
hair. The significance of a shaven head was that the person concerned was suffering, either through bereavement or disgrace, or
possibly both. Ezekiel probably felt keenly that he was suffering
along with the Lord through the deadness of God's people and the
disgrace they had brought upon His name.

Having given himself a haircut and shave with his dangerous,
ungainly implement, Ezekiel weighed his shorn locks and heaped
his hair into three piles. The first pile he threw in the fire and
soon the acrid smell of burning hair filled the nostrils of the
people. Then he took his sword and began to hack furiously at
the second pile. Having done that, he carefully picked out a few
hairs from the remaining pile and threw the rest of the hair up
in the air where the wind from the desert whipped it away. He put
some of the hairs in a fold in his tunic; he threw the rest into the
fire (5:2-4).

Misrepresenting God

The crowd dispersed and Ezekiel returned indoors. Still there was no word from his lips. Only these strangely disturbing, dramatic actions. Vivid and unavoidable and desperately unsettling. The Lord had told Ezekiel that his actions conveyed the appalling fact that a third of the people of Jerusalem would perish in the city, a third would be destroyed outside the city, and the final third, with the exception of a few people, would be scattered to the four winds (5:12).

Ezekiel may have found the drastic nature of divine judgment upon Jerusalem hard to understand, but the Lord explained something of great importance to the prophet. He told Ezekiel that He regarded Jerusalem as being in the "midst of the nations and countries that are round about her" (5:5). Jerusalem and her people were central to God's purposes and were placed in the middle of the nations as a model. The Jews in Jerusalem were highly privileged in that God had chosen them and their city to be the special place of His dwelling and the seat of His reign. The surrounding nations were only allowed to look and learn from the privileged people.

Privileged people, however, are the ones who bear the responsibilities. The incontrovertible fact of Jerusalem's inexcusable failure and rebellion necessitated an equally incontrovertible action of God in judgment. The people of God who sin publicly and thereby delude and confuse the public, must expect drastic and public action from the God they have so grossly misrepresented.

This divine principle appears to be little understood in the Church today. The very institution of God on earth, the Church of Jesus Christ, apparently thinks she can carelessly misrepresent God and anticipate nothing other than the ongoing grace and benevolence of God. To think like this is to ignore the principles of God's dealings with His ancient people and also to overlook the specific teachings of our Lord Jesus and the saga of Church history.

In His letters to the seven churches of Asia Minor, the Risen Lord warned that He would not hesitate to "remove the candlestick" (Rev. 2:5) of their witness if they did not get around to being what they were born to be. I have poked around in the ruins of Ephesus and in that beautiful area of modern Turkey I found nothing remotely resembling the Church of Jesus Christ. In fact, search as you will around the whole area and you will find only dead remnants of former glory. Travel across North Africa, the scene of much Early Church triumph, Christian scholarship, and glorious ministry, and you will find only lampstands. In many areas of Europe the same thing is true, and some see the same things beginning to happen in the 20th-century church in North America.

Could one say that God prefers to be unrepresented rather than misrepresented?

The Loosened Tongue

One day the Lord released the tongue of His prophet. "Son of man, set thy face towards the mountains of Israel and prophesy against them" (6:2). At last he was given the green light to open his mouth and explain the significance of his actions. The words came in a veritable torrent as he faced the west and addressed himself to the faraway land of Israel. The "mountains" were significant because it was on the "high places" that the people of Israel were engaging in illicit worship which was particularly displeasing to the Lord.

When God's people had arrived from Egypt, they cleared the land of pagan influence and took over the sites of pagan worship and adapted them to the worship of Jehovah. Eventually, the Lord had directed that the place of His abode would be Jerusalem, and efforts had been made repeatedly to turn the people from their mountaintop worship places to the place that was uniquely representative of God. Not that there was anything intrinsically wrong with worship on a mountaintop! But unfortunately, the Israelites sometimes used the pagan shrines and even the pillars which some commentators think were gross phallic symbols identified with the Canaanite fertility rites. God wanted His people out because they were trying to worship Him through methods and symbols that were totally opposed to Him.

This has always been a problem when man has worked out his own methods of worship and service, and ignored or rejected God's requirements. It isn't that God is given to nit-picking; it's just that He sees how easy it is for fallible people to use anti-God principles to try to show how pro-God they are.

Throughout the Israelites' history, God had repeatedly asked His people to destroy the "high places." There had been isolated responses, but nothing definite had ever been done. So God finally announced that if they wouldn't, he would! "Your altars will be desolate, and your images shall be broken; and I will cast down your bones around your altars" (see Ezekiel 6:4). It all sounds quite gruesome, but the significance is that once dead bodies had lain in a "holy place," that place could not be regarded as holy anymore. So in His drastic intervention, God was going to close down once and for all what His people had failed repeatedly to close down.

They Shall Know

Four times in the sixth chapter the expression, "they shall know I am the Lord," is used, and it obviously is important to the Lord's explanation of His actions. God's prime concern at all times, as we have already seen, is that people everywhere should know that He is Lord. God is committed to do whatever it takes to safeguard the clear presentation of His Lordship, and He looks to His people to be similarly committed to correctly representing His Lordship. It is easy to say this, but to consider what it may entail is almost overwhelming.

What would happen if we took seriously our high calling to accurately project that "He is Lord," both in terms of the message we present and the functions of the church through which we try to present it? We might discover that some of our practices and methods are more closely aligned to the spirit of the world than the Spirit of Christ.

How do we approach the pastor of another church when we want him to come to us? What incentives do we offer him? What rosy pictures do we paint? How many skeletons do we keep in the ecclesiastical closet?

Some astute observers of the church scene may have noticed that churches are sometimes not very good at having the Lord as Lord of their finances, and have decided that the church's Lord is basically a graduate of the Harvard Business School. Suppose the church got wind of this criticism and said in a specially called meeting, "Our financial structure owes more to deficit financing than dependent faith. This is not a fair projection of the One who we say is Lord, so the motion before the church is that we reorganize our financial structure to more accurately project our concept of His Lordship." That would create quite a furor, wouldn't it? But it is something that we as the Lord's people ought to courageously explore.

The Remnant

The exiles listened as the prophet continued to address himself to the mountains of Israel. The intensity of his message and the power of his projection must have been greatly increased by the fact that he was breaking his long silence with such devastating words. The predictions of doom were unrelenting till suddenly he quoted a beautiful word from the Lord. "Yet I will leave a remnant, that ye may have some that shall escape the sword among the nations when ye shall be scattered through the countries" (6:8). Remember the few hairs that he carefully took from the third pile and tucked in the fold of his tunic? They were representative of the remnant that God was committed to keep.

God has never left Himself without a witness. Even at the time of deep societal rebellion and disintegration which led to the Flood, there was Noah and his family (see Gen. 6:1-8). Elijah remained faithful in the midst of unfaithfulness and discovered there was a much bigger remnant that he thought. He moaned, "I even I only am left," but he was wrong! (See 1 Kings 19:14-18.) God has His people in Soviet Russia and His Church in Red China. Even in countries like Nepal where it is a crime to be a Christian, He has His servants. They are around somewhere even if, according to the authorities, they aren't supposed to be there! He has His people among the Gypsies of France, the communes of California, the high places in Washington, and Death Row in many prisons.

They are there to remember who He is, to reflect on His faithfulness, to mourn their prevailing unfaithfulness, and to know that He is Lord so truly that they will make Him known to others.

Hand Clapping and Foot Stomping

God's man in Tel-abib was always ready with a little surprise. After he had burst into a torrent of words after his long and silent vigil, Ezekiel suddenly took off in a good old foot-stomping, hand-clapping (6:11) rhythm. Once he'd got the rhythm to his liking and the attention of the crowd to his satisfaction, he started to prophesy again (6:11-14). Perhaps the prophecy facing Israel had begun to lose its impact, so he got word from the Lord that it was time to liven up the proceedings. He didn't say anything particularly new, but no doubt some who hadn't got the message the first time around couldn't miss it the second time!

The End

Again "the word of the Lord" came to him (7:1). It is tempting to try to surmise in what way the word came to him, but as we are given no details, presumably it is either not important or we are not expected to know. What matters is that God spoke to him and he passed on the word. "An end, the end is come" (7:2).

After years of patience and centuries of forebearing, the time had run out. The Lord announced that it would be counterproductive for Him to give further opportunities for repentance. The time had come when, in the Lord's view, He would begin to undermine His justice if He continued to express His mercy. The time had come for the Lord to do what He had been promising to do because if He held off any longer, people would assume He either didn't mean what He said or couldn't do what He promised. For either of these things to happen would be a disaster of major proportions. Better to pour out judgment on the unrepentant than to give opportunity to the unrepentant to think that the Omnipotent has become impotent. Better to run the risk of God being castigated as a cruel God than have the people think that He must have died because He hasn't done anything for so long.

"Makkeh"

But do not fail to see that even at the point of the "end" when God says, "All right, that's it," He still warns before He acts. There is no such thing as the judgment of God without warning, and there is never judgment without evidence of mercy. If the Book of Ezekiel in these early, difficult chapters reminds us of nothing else, it speaks forcibly to the fact of God's remarkable dealings with the people He has made. Dealings that are designed to draw them to Himself in life-styles of trust, love, and satisfaction. Dealings that promise forgiveness and mercy even in the administration of justice and judgment.

In the middle of the statement the Lord announced Himself by a striking title, "Jehovah-makkeh"—the Lord who strikes (7:9)! John Taylor states "To hearers and readers who were used to the names of God like 'Jehovah-jireh' and 'Jehovah-nissi' it must have come home with tremendous force to have Him described as 'Jehovah-makkeh'. The Lord who had provided and protected was about to strike."

In our need to know the Lord and His desire for us to know

that He is the Lord, we must never be allowed to forget that Jehovah is "makkeh" as truly as He is "jireh" and "nissi." To leave out any aspect of His revealed Being is to paint an unsatisfactory picture. It's rather like an artist determining to paint a woodland scene of light and shadow but arbitrarily deciding to use no black or grey and trying to portray the full glory of the scene with only pinks and greens.

Disintegration

Details of the "end" that the people were to anticipate in the very near future showed that moral, financial, and social disintegration was inevitable (7:10-27). All they had held dear would fall apart. The things they had trusted would fold up and disappear. The things in which they had taken delight would become unpleasant and irrelevant, and the things that had filled their thinking and captivated their attention would be shown to be useless in their hour of real trouble. The end was about to arrive and when the Lord finally chose to act, nobody and nothing could stand it one moment longer.

These words were a salutary warning for those who in Israel's history had presumed on God's mercy. It is an equally salutary note for those who today assume that disaster could never befall those who rebel and resist God as thoroughly and relentlessly as those to whom Ezekiel spoke.

This interesting and disturbing passage of God's Word has brought three things home to my mind with great force.

1. There is an absolute integrity about God's Word to man that must be preserved at all cost. That God has spoken to our world is beyond dispute. That our world needs to know exactly what He has said is equally obvious. But that the world is not really getting a full picture of who He is and what He has said is plain. To a great extent, the blame for this must be laid at the door of those who seek to present a message that will be more acceptable than accurate. For the simple fact of the matter is that some of the inescapable truth of God is particularly unpalatable. Therefore, it behooves the Church to check carefully to see if the word we are getting out is such that people will know that "He is the Lord" in all the varied aspect of His Being.

2. There is a remarkable flexibility about the way that God is prepared to communicate with man. Take Ezekiel's ministry as we

have followed it through the early stages. He used graphic art, he engaged in dramatic actions, he used rhythmic dance, pronounced oracles, and recited poetry! Not bad for a man just getting started without any chalkboards, overhead projectors, flood lighting or budgets! The Lord taught Ezekiel what He impressed upon Paul many years later. "All means" should be used to "win some" (1 Cor. 9:22).

3. God insists that His men should recognize their expendability. To put it bluntly, the message matters more than the messengers. Those who recognize this have no argument with it even though they know they will probably be called upon to prove their acceptance in practical, sometimes painful ways.

Ezekiel's experience at this point should encourage each of us to check on the integrity of our message, the flexibility of our methods, and the expendability of ourselves as messengers.

6

The Hole in the Wall

Ezekiel 8—11

For about 14 months Ezekiel "spoke" to the people through his strange dramatic portrayals and his occasional outbursts of speech. At first he was undoubtedly regarded as something of an oddity, but in time the leadership of the community began to take seriously what he had to say.

One day the elders came to his house and "sat before" him, probably enquiring whether Ezekiel had a word from the Lord. It is interesting to note that the people of the Exile had not completely fallen apart. They had organized their own leadership and were making some effort to carry on their accustomed routine, though it must have been extremely difficult and often very discouraging.

While the elders were sitting in Ezekiel's house, "the hand of the Lord fell upon" the prophet (8:1). Immediately he was transported into another of his visionary experiences. How long it lasted we do not know. Whether the elders sat around and waited we don't know either.

It should be pointed out that while today it would be very strange if somebody went off into a trance as we sought his advice, there was nothing uncommon about the procedure in Ezekiel's time. It would certainly play havoc with a counselor's carefully planned 45-minute schedule of appointments if he needed this kind of input before he could give some counsel. His secretary would be driven frantic. Imagine having to delay appointments indefinitely until the counselor "came back!" Or having to answer the phone with, "I'm sorry, but the counselor just stepped out of the office and was last seen heading for Jerusalem, either in the body or out of it."

Image of Jealousy

The "form of a hand" lifted Ezekiel by the hair and carried him between heaven and earth to Jerusalem. The "form of a hand" belonged to the One who glowed like fire, none other than the Lord of the throne, although notice how strangely vague is the description that Ezekiel gives (8:3). Immediately he was deposited at the north gate of the inner court of the Temple. The north gate, also called the "altar gate," was adjacent to the king's palace and was particularly important because it was used by the king.

At this strategic place, Ezekiel stood in his vision and what he saw sent a chill through his frame. Right there by the inner court where kings entered the temple area and where sacrifices were brought to the altar, the people had placed "the image of jealousy" (8:3). What the image was we do not know, though some researchers believe it was a carved slab of stone depicting various mythological scenes related to the pagan gods and their activities. Whatever it was, it provoked the Lord to jealousy.

Our understanding of jealousy is such that we sometimes have trouble thinking of God stooping to such an unworthy, immature attitude. But God had shown that He was a jealous God in the law that He had given through Moses to the people. It was not that God was immature and threatened by opposition, but that anything that contradicted Him was error and anything erroneous was detrimental to His people. He could not take a "broad view" of error any more than He could have a tolerant attitude toward iniquity. To do either would be to jeopardize His own integrity and ultimately confound and confuse the people even more.

Nevertheless, the image that was so contradictory to all that God had revealed of Himself stood immediately adjacent to "the glory of the Lord." From our vantage point of being far removed from the scene and with the benefit of that most valuable asset called "hindsight," we are appalled that those in charge of the temple would allow the "glory" and the "image" to be in the same place. Yet perhaps we are not far enough removed from our own situation to be able to see that there may be areas in our worship where we expect the Lord to share His place with the things that contradict His very being and nature.

Creeping Things

The people of Jerusalem were great syncretists. They loved to bring the things of other gods alongside the things of God. Perhaps they did it in the name of a liberal attitude or a broad-minded approach. It may have been that they were quite prepared to bring in any religious conviction alongside their own rather than upset any group by rejecting what they had to offer.

Such an attitude is increasingly prevalent in the Church today. There are those who in the name of scholarship advocate the assimilation of "truths" that contradict Scripture and in the name of love urge the acceptance of things which God has condemned. Taking a stand against these apparently loving and tolerant attitudes often goes over like a lead balloon, and yet failing to oppose them may be fatal to the ongoing of the work of the Lord.

The One guiding Ezekiel drew his attention to the "image" and expressed utter disgust. An "abomination" He called it, and added that its presence there demanded the withdrawal of the Lord's presence because the two could not coexist (8:6). Détente was not a possibility in this situation! God said, "If you are appalled by the 'image of jealousy' you haven't seen anything yet!"

Leading him to one of the doors which is not identified, Ezekiel's Guide pointed to a hole in the wall. "Dig the hole bigger, Ezekiel, and see what you can see." Ezekiel began to dig and eventually uncovered a secret door. He threw the door open and found himself in a large, crowded room full of clouds of sickly incense.

Over 70 men, some of whom Ezekiel recognized, were in the room, worshiping all kinds of engravings which covered the walls of the room. Probably the "creeping things and abominable beasts and idols" (8:10) pictured there were related to the familiar serpent deities of Egypt. How the people of Israel, who had known the exploits of Jehovah throughout their history, could be interested in serpent gods and pagan practices is hard for us to understand unless we realize that there was probably considerable political motivation behind the activity. The elders may have been engaged in this kind of worship in an attempt to build up good relations with nations they felt might be able to help them in their national and political problems.

God Is Dead?

Perhaps the Jews felt a bit guilty about this because they were doing it "in the dark." Yet they were salving their consciences by trying to persuade each other that "the Lord seeth us not; the Lord hath forsaken the earth" (8:12). In other words, their theology was a "God is dead" theology. In the place of the God they thought had quit the scene, they had looked to all kinds of religious and political powers that hopefully could do for them what Jehovah had failed to do. God called this an abomination even worse than the "image of jealousy."

Parallels are not difficult to find in today's spiritual arena. Some of the Lord's people are in danger of putting politics in the place of worship and leaning more upon the political process than upon the Lord. Is it possible that the Lord would intervene in the affairs of a nation which has known the truth of God for years and through its history has increasingly neglected that truth? God still reserves the right to judge even the most favored people!

There is an increasing tendency to incorporate into the spiritual life of the church a political emphasis designed to thwart what may be judgment of God in the form of political, economic, and social disintegration. Could it not be that the political climate of some countries which have allowed great freedom to worship and serve God may be changing because God is disappointed with the abuse of this freedom? Why should God not allow the political climate to change as a judgment on an irresponsible nation? If He does act in this way, it is useless for Christians to affiliate with political forces aligned against the one that the Christians fear will jeopardize their freedom. The problem has more to do with the judgment of God than with the spread of political ideology. Political answers will not suffice; only spiritual values will avail. God calls political attempts by His people to solve spiritual problems an abomination," if for no other reason than they are a veiled denial of God's right to judge an unrepentant nation and an attempt to avert well-merited judgment.

Tammuz

There were more abominations for Ezekiel to see. Outside the walls of the temple area the women were doing their thing—they were more open than the men! They were worshiping "Tammuz" (8:14). Tammuz, a pagan god of nature, had been imported to make up what was presumably lacking in Jehovah. A large part of the worship of Tammuz, which was closely related to ideas of vegetation and fertility, was mourning that he had died and become the god of the underworld. His followers planted gardens where they wept for and worshiped him. Isaiah may have alluded to this when he referred to the people's futile gardening efforts (Isa. 17:10-11).

At the risk of overdoing it, I suggest that we so emphasize eating the right things and growing the right kinds of foods presumably so that we can all live happily ever after that we are in danger of forgetting the God of our salvation. He is the One who provides the food and preserves and protects us. Getting slightly "kooky" about what and how we cook may just be an evidence of God being put even further back on the shelf.

Sun Worship

Ezekiel's attention was next directed to the area "between the porch and the altar" (8:16), reserved for priests and Levites. There about 25 men, priests, and Levites, men of great position and privilege, were worshiping the sun with their backs to the temple. This was a blatant denial of the very place on which they stood and the very service they professed to perform. It was the ultimate insult to Jehovah. The men called to lead the people in the worship and service of God were not only failing to do this but were directing the attention of the people away from Jehovah and encouraging them to worship the created more than the Creator.

The worship of the creature has always been a problem for those who want to worship the living and true God. He, being invisible, is often overlooked because of the undeniable magnificence of the visible things He has created. Nevertheless, as Paul clearly pointed out to the Romans, those who serve "the creature more than the Creator" are "changing the truth of God into a lie" and that is the most heinous sin (Rom. 1:25).

The Seven Men

The Lord expostulated to Ezekiel and instructed with a loud voice that those responsible for the city should present themselves before the Lord with "destroying weapons in their hands" (9:2). Seven men appeared promptly. Six carried "slaughter weapons" and the seventh, dressed in linen clothes, carried writing materials. They stood silently beside the altar. At this point of the vision, the "glory of the Lord" (that is, the visible evidence of His presence in the midst of His people) left the cherubim and the wheels and the platform and the throne and appeared at the door of the temple.

The man with the writing materials was ordered to go throughout Jerusalem looking for people who were distressed by the people's rejection of the Lord and who openly cried in bitterness and repentance at the apostasy on every hand. On the forehead of each of these people he was to place "a mark" (9:4). The other six men were commanded to go throughout the city and destroy everyone who did not have the mark.

In this vision the horrified Ezekiel was being shown both the promised judgment of God on unrepentant people and the protecting power of God over those whose hearts were moved toward Him.

Sign of the Cross

A fascinating fact about the mark on the forehead can be missed easily. The mark stipulated was the last letter of the Hebrew alphabet, called *taw* and written X. The sign of the cross was the mark which freed the people from the wrath of God and brought them under the protection of God! Perhaps this is coincidence, but it is more probable that in this application of the X is a foretaste of the message of salvation through the blood of the Cross. The early Christian commentators certainly thought this was the case.

There is no suggestion that Ezekiel understood this, but we do know that on some occasions, people in the biblical record said things, the significance of which they themselves did not understand. For instance, Caiaphas, the high priest, said that "one should die for the people and that the whole nation perish not . . ." without realizing that he was making a momentous statement of the substitutionary atonement. As John said, he made this announcement "not of himself" (John 11:50-51). He was actually prophesying something he didn't believe!

H. L. Ellison in his book, *Ezekiel, The Man And His Message,* said, "This is one of the many examples where Hebrew prophets spoke better than they knew." Understanding this principle of Scripture opens the door to realizing that "coincidences" may be special, subtle touches from the Lord to give added authenticity to His revelation of Himself.

Where Judgment Begins

The seven men were to "begin at my sanctuary" (9:6). The Lord stipulated that the awful judgment was to begin at the place where the repentance ought to have begun. Judgment would fall first on the temple, the place of worship where men called of God were to minister daily to the Lord and lead His people in humble, obedient worship. These men, however, had been misleading the people and confusing them by their own overt rebellion and cynical disregard of God's principles of behavior.

Peter was also alert to this principle of divine operation. He said, "Judgment must begin at the house of God" (1 Peter 4:17). It is clear that he meant that Christians could anticipate persecution which, in some instances, would bear aspects of God's judgment. His judgment of His people is not designed to rob them of their status as His children, but rather to bring them to the kind of commitment to Him that brings glory to Him and equips them more thoroughly for His service.

It is a sobering thought that God's dissatisfaction with a nation's rejection of Him may be first expressed among the believers because they have been partially responsible for the nation's rejection. When the Church becomes inconsistent in witness, fails to function as the salt of society, and begins to conform more and more to the standards of the world system, a society has lost the most reliable corrective influence available to it. How great, therefore, is the responsibility of the Church and how necessary is the pruning and corrective work of the Lord, even in judgment.

Tough and Tender

It is refreshing to note that Ezekiel was not insensitive to the plight of those upon whom the judgment would fall. Hard foreheads do not preclude soft hearts. But maintaining the balance of hardness and softness is one of the most difficult aspects of the ministry!

Some people can touch your hearts with their "sob stories" and take you to the cleaners emotionally, financially, and even morally. Many a soft-hearted Christian has been ruined by a calculating rascal. Yet, at the same time, many tough-minded servants of God have been so cynical of those who have deep problems and so insensitive to the pain they are feeling, that their brusque refusal to get involved has only served to exacerbate the problem and deepen the wounds.

It is my constant prayer that I might learn how to be "tough and tender" with those to whom I minister. My wife is a great help at this point. What I lack in tenderness she often lacks in toughness, so we have a working relationship which goes something like this. If she feels that I have been insensitive or too tough, she says so and gives me practical suggestions as to how I might remedy the situation. On the other hand, I help her by pointing out when she is being far too soft and that if she continues to be naive she will be incapable of helping the people for whom she feels such concern. They will not get from her the unvarnished truth which they need to avoid unreality and self-induced fantasy. This kind of partnership in living is not only necessary in ministry, but in every area of relationships.

The Severity of God

Having completed the work which impressed on Ezekiel's consciousness the inevitability and severity of the impending judgment, the six men faded from the vision and once again, the chariot-throne of the Lord of glory took center stage. Ezekiel again described it in considerable detail, perhaps to emphasize that he had added little new to the descriptions already given. Nevertheless, he was once more overwhelmed with the presence of God.

The record reminds us that we should be as overwhelmed with a revelation of the severity of God as we are with a vision of His majesty or His mercy. However, believers often don't want to know about this aspect of His nature. When they are confronted with the idea of God's judgment, they usually react with questions rather than responding with reverent worship.

The Glory Departed

The man with the linen suit reported back to the Lord and was promptly instructed to go in between the wheels of the chariot-throne, take some of the coals burning therein, and scatter the burning embers over the city (10:1-2).

The drama preceded a startling set of events. The glory of the Lord departed from the holy place. As we will see, the significance of this movement was that it was the beginning of the long-threatened removal of the visible evidence of God's presence among His people. This removal took place in stages. First, it moved from the holy place to the outside of the temple (10:18). This gave the people the opportunity to see more of the Lord's presence than they had ever seen. But it made no difference. Then, along with the chariot-throne, the Glory moved to the mountain on the east side of Jerusalem, and stayed there as if brooding over the city.

There is no mention of the departure of the Glory from the Mount of Olives, but much later Ezekiel saw the Glory returning from the east. This has led some commentators to believe that the glory of the Lord was removed from sinful Jerusalem and placed in the camp of the exiles. Others suggest that it remained on the Mount as if to remind the people that the Glory was gone from the temple and the city where it belonged, but ready to return when the people turned back to God.

Meat in the Pot

While Ezekiel was watching the slow, deliberate movement of the Glory, the Lord directed his attention to a group of 25 men who were meeting outside the East gate (11:1). They were people who had been most influential in forging the attitudes of the unrepentant city. They insisted, "It is not near" (11:3). By that they were probably saying, "Don't listen to the prophets of doom. All is well, there is nothing to fear. Go ahead and build your houses, and live the good life. Sure, things are bad around here, but we are all right. We are like meat cooking in a pot over the fire. The fire can't get to us, so cheer up and watch us win through this whole tricky situation." This seems to have been their message, and Ezekiel was told to refute it. He proceeded to do so in graphic language. "You think you are safe in your cauldron, but I want you to know that this city is not safe, and you are not going to survive. The cauldron will be overthrown and you will be cast out and destroyed" (11:5-12).

Immediately after Ezekiel had finished speaking, one of the leaders, a man named Pelatiah, dropped dead in the middle of the group. This was too much for Ezekiel. He fell down before the Lord and cried, "Lord, how much longer is this going on? Haven't You gone far enough?" (11:13)

It's interesting to see how quick-witted Ezekiel was in taking the analogy the rebels were using to prove their safety and turning it around to prove the opposite. This is the mark of a good communicator of the truth of God. But all good communicators have to learn that giving the message cleverly and in striking fashion is one thing, living with the results is another. It is only when we see the awe-inspiring results of what we are saying for God that we are rescued from being clever and slick in our presentations and become increasingly real and irrefutable in our pronouncements on the Lord's behalf.

A Little Sanctuary

Jehovah's answer to the overwrought prophet's question was as prompt as it was surprising. He said, "Ezekiel, I have scattered My people among the nations. They have been banished from the land I gave them because they have failed to be what I planned for them to be. But I have not deserted them and will be 'a little sanctuary' to them even in their exile. They can still know Me there even as you have known Me in Tel-abib. Moreover, Ezekiel, I want you to understand that I have every intention of bringing them back into this land so that when they have learned their lessons they can have the opportunity of being, once again, My people as I am their God. They will once more have the chance to function as My chosen ones. The world needs to see Me operating in the midst of My people. So I will restore them, and they shall be My people and I will be their God" (11:15-18).

Immediately after the promise of Judgment, the promise of restoration is given. God, the God of justice and fierce wrath, is also a God of long-suffering, patience, love, and tender-hearted compassion.

New Hearts for Old

The Lord went on to say what all the world needs to hear. "The problem with My people, Ezekiel, is a heart problem. They need new, warm and tender hearts toward Me in the place of those hard, cold hearts that beat in their puffed-out chests and drive them on in their senseless independence and rebellion. I will give new hearts to those who will let Me. I will change their inner attitudes and mould their desires to My desires. Their interests and their aspirations will be revolutionized and I will restore My people to a life of service and worship through an inner revolution of loving-obedience" (11:19-20).

Here the message of the Lord becomes even clearer through His tough but tender dealings with His people. The principle is unchanging and indeed unchangeable. Sin brings judgment; independence bears the fruit of disintegration. Rebellion turns people from God and God from people. No external antidote is available to remedy the ills of any individual or society that knows only outright rebellion and independence from and hostility to the Eternal God.

A new heart is needed and God is in the heart transplant business. He specializes in taking the cold, unregenerate heart and infusing into it the life of His Spirit, the reality of His love, and the warmth of His presence. God also gives His cool or lukewarm children a fresh touch of His Spirit and His erring churches a fresh exposure to Himself which, if they respond positively, brings about a new glow of devotion and a fiery determination to serve Him. I believe this is the reviving and renewing work our society needs. Our God is ready to do it in His Church and through the Church in society.

Some time ago, a young lady came to my study to ask what the Bible says about divorce. I opened the Scriptures to her and said, "God hates it, but will 'suffer' it under certain circumstances."

Eagerly she asked, "What are the circumstances?"

"You must have a hard heart," I replied.

"My husband is no good," she said. "He won't work, he won't take me out, he bores me. I don't like what he likes, and he doesn't like what I like. I have no alternative but to admit I made a mistake and get out as quick as I can."

"What about your hard heart?" I asked rather pointedly.

"I don't have a hard heart," she replied. "It's him. He's the one who's got the hard heart."

"That's funny," I replied. "I could have sworn I detected some resentment in your voice and some antagonism toward your husband. I must have been wrong, but I thought I could sense an unforgiving spirit and an unwilling attitude. Are you sure that he's the only one with a hard heart in your family?"

"Well, I'm not going to pretend to you that I'm perfect," she admitted somewhat lamely.

"I didn't say anything about perfection," I insisted. "I was talking about your hard heart."

"All right," she said. "Maybe I have a hard heart, but I've tried and there's nothing I can do about it. I've no alternative."

"I think you're right. If you insist on keeping your hard heart, there really is no alternative but marital breakdown. But there is an alternative to a hard heart."

"Huh? What's the alternative to a hard heart?"

"I thought you'd never ask! You'll never guess. It's a soft heart, tender and warm."

"And where do you think I'm going to get one of those?" she asked with a suspicious tone in her voice.

"Ezekiel," I replied.

To make a long and beautiful story short, the young lady received from the Lord Jesus the sort of thing that Jehovah promised His rebellious, hard-hearted people. She received a new heart, began to live in the power of the Holy Spirit in obedience to God's commands to love. Later her husband also got a new heart. Today they minister effectively in our fellowship, and the people in their neighborhood are discovering that God is their God and they are His people.

God hasn't changed a bit. He's still in the people-changing business, but He won't put up with rebellion or excuse sin.

As the words of the Lord were silenced and the vision slowly faded, Ezekiel felt himself being returned to Tel-abib. He was a changed man, one who had been confronted with God's truth. As he returned from his trance and came back to the dusty reality of his own house, were the elders still drinking his coffee? I don't know, but I'm sure that he couldn't wait to tell the whole story to all the people. I wonder where he started. How did he explain the awfulness of the divine wrath and the tenderness of divine forgiveness?

7

Eyes to See
and Ears to Hear

Ezekiel 12—17

Despite all the messages and dramatic presentations by the "son
of man," the people of Tel-abib were not convinced. They had
seen much and heard plenty, but seeing, they had not seen, and
hearing, they had not heard. Not an uncommon situation! It is not
unusual for the truth we see to be erased from our spiritual consciousness almost immediately and for the words we profess to
hear to be quickly superseded by the next sound that comes along.

The phenomenon is partly due to the "blinding" work of the
Enemy of souls who by a variety of methods nullifies the full
impact of what we see or hear. Sometimes he exaggerates the
image or impression to the point of making it ludicrous. We immediately dismiss it. Or he distracts us with another piece of more
interesting information. The original piece of information which
may well have been the most important is then overshadowed by
something more attractive but less important.

The main problem with our failure to assimilate truth is the
will. It is true that we are easily distracted and that we are constantly receiving information, but we all have a great deal of
trouble with putting into action the things we know!

The people of Tel-abib wouldn't have had too many distractions
in the camp, but they hadn't seen what they had seen, or heard
what they had heard. The reason was their rebellious hearts,
which prevented them from acting on the truth.

I have often heard people say, "I went to a good church for 20 years and never heard the Gospel. My minister never preached Christ and the 'way of salvation' was never explained." My reaction to this kind of statement is to remind the people concerned that their preacher undoubtedly had his faults, but the possibility of his *never* giving a hint of the necessity of commitment to Christ and trust in Him during a period of 20 years is quite unlikely. It is much more probable that the complaining person gave such superficial attention to the pastor's message that it was easy for him to be "blinded." There is also the very real possibility that he had a heart that was resistant to the truth.

Pack Your Bags

One day God told the "son of man" to start packing and to do it in full daylight. This must have been quite amusing for the people and extremely embarrassing for Ezekiel. He was packing for a journey with nowhere to go! And everybody knew he had nowhere to go. Making sure the Tel-abibans were watching, Ezekiel knocked a hole in the wall of his house. Since it was made of sun-dried mud bricks, it was not difficult to knock a few out of place. I doubt that he was too popular with his wife! After climbing through the wall and picking up his meager belongings, our hero blindfolded himself and trudged off into the sunset! (12:3-6)

The Lord told Ezekiel that he was a "sign" to the people of the camp and the whole house of Israel. Obediently and at great personal cost and inconvenience, the prophet fulfilled his instructions to the letter. He wrote, with beautiful simplicity, "And I did so as I was commanded" (12:6-7).

The next morning God explained the strange instructions. (It's good to remind ourselves that obedience often has to wait for reasons—sometimes a long, long time!) "Ezekiel, the people have been asking you what you're doing. Tell them that you have enacted what is going to happen to the people of Jerusalem. They will be taken away into captivity with their meager refugee belongings on their shoulders. Their king, Zedekiah, will try to make a run for it during the night by digging through the city wall. He will be disguised with a blindfold but he will not escape. I will see to that. He will be carried away to Babylon, but he will never see it because he will die" (12:9-13).

The exact meaning of Jehovah's words to Ezekiel is somewhat

unclear, but it is certain that in general they were a prediction concerning the fate of Jerusalem and in particular of Zedekiah. These things actually happened to him, as we know from the account in 2 Kings 25:1-8.

Trophies
Some of the people would be allowed to escape, for which the Lord gave a striking reason. If the world saw the kind of people who were coming out of Jerusalem, everyone would clearly understand why the Lord was so upset. In fact, these unsavory people, scattering into distant places, would be messengers of the Lord in a perverse sort of way (12:16). They would not be trophies of His grace but living illustrations of the rightness of His judgment. People would look at them and say, "I'm not surprised God judged them, they sure needed it. I'm surprised He held off so long, but I'm glad to see that He doesn't tolerate their kind of behavior."

Again we see that God insists on making clear that He is the Lord. Those who respond to Him demonstrate His saving power, while those who reject Him show forth His eternal justice. Moreover, the fact of the fulfilled predictions concerning Jerusalem and Zedekiah would enhance the reputation of the Lord's prophet because he had shown the veracity of the Word of the Lord. In every way the Lord was being glorified.

The Quaker
Acting on instructions, Ezekiel began to put on a real show when he ate his breakfast. He started to shiver outsize shivers and quake in his sandals as he ate his starvation rations.

"What's wrong now, Ezekiel?" his ever-present watchers asked.

"The people of the doomed city will eat what little food they have with fear and trembling. I don't think you realize how serious this whole thing is. I wish I could impress upon you the immensity of the impending disaster. Stark tragedy is staring the people of Jerusalem in the face," he replied (12:19).

"Come on now, Ezekiel" the Tel-abibans retorted, "you don't expect us to believe that, do you? You know the old proverb, 'Time passes and these visions never come to anything!'"

Ezekiel replied, "The Lord's response to that is 'Time's up and this time the vision will be effective' " (12:22-23).

It may seem remarkable to us that people still would not heed the warning, yet a quick glance at history shows that man has rarely taken seriously what God has predicted. The attitude of Tel-abib is the basic attitude of the world today. It has a built-in refusal to accept the fact that God will ultimately intervene.

When He intervenes, however, it is a different matter. Among the Jewish exiles there would be a change of heart when the judgment really came, just as there was a dramatic response to what God had said through Noah. But it was a classic case of "too little, too late!"

Such a response is true even of the redeemed members of the body of Christ. Dire predictions about the consequences of disobedience or perpetual disregard of divine principles are usually taken "with a pinch of salt." But as we have seen, God does not hesitate to act when He finds it necessary. To think that He won't do it "this time" is to make a particularly dangerous assumption!

Now I Will Act

Some of the people, unable to refute what Ezekiel was saying, yet not wanting to believe it, took the middle course.

"Well," they said, "I'm sure you're right, Ezekiel. It's obvious that one of these days God may well intervene. To deny that possibility would be to deny God the right to be God and we would never do that, but we must say that it is highly unlikely that this will happen in our generation" (see 12:27).

To this the Lord bluntly replied, "There will be no prolongation of what I have said. What I have spoken is spoken, and now I will act" (see 12:28).

The attitude of the people is in some ways understandable. For years they had been ministered to by a lot of prophetic quacks. There had been a dreary procession of people who had talked the ears off the populace saying they had a word from the Lord, but nothing had ever happened. They predicted all manner of things but what they had to say was more the product of their imagination than divine revelation. The Lord called them "foxes in the deserts" (13:3-4).

Whitewash

The "foxes" line had been attractive and had produced a great response. "Peace" was their message. The only thing wrong with this beautiful theme was that it was a lie (13:5-10). Isn't it terrible that a beautiful and inspiring promise can be turned into a horrendous lie?

Perhaps nothing is more damaging to the people of God than a prophet who tells his hearers what they want to hear at the expense of what they need to hear. Messengers of peace who in time of conflict say what God has not said build edifices that inevitably crumble. The Lord scathingly categorized such people's ministry as the building of shoddy, flimsy, whitewashed walls (13:10). The finished effect looked great, but the Lord said He would send a downpour that would remove the whitewash, reveal the shoddy, inadequate nature of the work, and make the whole thing crumble (13:11-16). If people hear inadequate presentations of truth, such as peace, long enough, they may even come to the point of refusing the real thing when it comes along.

The exiled women had been producing their share of quacks too. They were specializing in various activities which the Lord called "hunting the souls of people" (13:17-18). He was saying categorically that these women with their "spiritual" activities were hurting the people they were professing to help. We are not certain what they were doing with their "pillows," "kerchiefs," "handfuls of barley," and "pieces of bread," but we know the Lord despised it (13:18-19). Evidently they were into some kind of "magic," perhaps with Babylonian overtones.

God's exposure of false teaching and learning and His displeasure with both is surely relevant today. He cares for the souls of men so much and resists all who would blind their understanding and sear their consciences, even to the point of destroying the ministers and the ministry of confusion.

The Good Guys

Having dealt in summary fashion with the proverbs that were popular in Tel-abib, the Lord then turned His attention to another "objection" that apparently was being leveled at Ezekiel's message. This line of reasoning went: "That God will judge someday we have no doubt, but while we have some righteous men in our midst, we will be all right because He would never destroy the righteous with the wicked."

To this the Lord instructed His man to respond, "Even if the Lord could find men of the caliber of Noah, Daniel, and Job in the city, it wouldn't alter what He has said. These men, in their relationship with the Lord, were men of high calling and great integrity, but they couldn't save another person. They were responsible to God for their own lives and God responded to them in terms of their attitudes to Him. Every individual is responsible to God and no individual can protect another from the consequences of his own sin." (See 14:14-15).

But people still cling to what they think are the transferable merits of the good guys! Some time ago, I was boarding an airliner when someone I didn't know came up to me and said, "You're Stuart Briscoe, aren't you?"

"So I've been led to believe," I replied.

"Oh, you've no idea how glad I am to see you," she said.

"Thank you very much, but why are you so glad to see me?"

"Because I'm terrified of flying but I know if you're on the flight, God will not allow anything to happen to it so I'll be quite safe."

Divine Vine

Along came another objection. "You don't seem to understand, Ezekiel. We are the chosen people. The vine. We exist to bring forth fruit among the nations. To show that God is Lord. He's committed to us, Ezekiel. He has cast His lot with us. Everybody knows we belong to Him and He would never let anything happen to His vineyard and His vine."

Ezekiel's answer was plainly uncomplimentary! Moses had written a poem about the Lord's people being a vine that brought forth "grapes of gall" (Deut. 32:32). Hosea said, "Israel is an empty vine" (Hos. 10:1). Isaiah wrote a similar song which included the heart-rending line, "Wherefore when I look that it should bring forth grapes, brought it forth wild grapes?" (Isa. 5:4) And Jeremiah had weighed in with the heavy statement, "I had planted thee a noble vine, wholly a right seed; how then art thou turned into the degenerate plant of a strange vine unto Me? (Jer. 2:21)

The theme was similar in all cases. Israel, chosen and cared for by God to bring forth much fruit that would glorify Him, had become barren and wild, sour and bitter.

Ezekiel continued the theme but went one step further. He didn't concentrate on the idea of Israel being a disappointment because of fruitlessness. He assumed that, and emphasized another aspect of the vine.

Everyone knows that vines are for bearing grapes, and if they don't do that, what on earth can they do? Vines that don't bear grapes simply clutter up the ground. Ezekiel made this point with great force. "Compare a vine to an oak. It is nothing. Can you use the wood of the vine to make furniture? No, it is impossible to work the wood. Then use it to make pegs on which we can hang our equipment. The pegs wouldn't be strong enough. Well, we can always use it for firewood. Try. It won't even burn, the ends will char but all you will get is smoke and smoldering. Vines without grapes are useless. Burned vines charred and smoldering are worse than useless.

"So will I make my chosen place Jerusalem, a burned out 'nothing' among the nations. Jerusalem, the place graced with My presence, blessed with My calling to bring forth fruit, has failed. Now it is useless to Me and will be even more useless when shortly it becomes a smoldering, smoking heap" (see 15:1-8).

True Vine

These morbid words have a glorious counterpoint in the New Testament. The Lord Jesus made the statement, "I am the true Vine" (John 15:1). The emphasis is on His true effectiveness as the Vine of God as opposed to the failure of Israel to be that Vine. All that Israel had failed to be, the Lord Jesus would be. In the fulness of His glory and the sinlessness of His being, He would show forth the praises of the One who sent Him. But there was to be an added dimension to the glorious ministry of the true Vine: His branches. He told His disciples that they were the branches (John 15:5).

Men and women in Christ are given the opportunity to be through Him what Israel had been called to be—they were to have been the human means through which the Lord would make Himself known. This is one of the most exciting things about being a Christian, a disciple of the true Vine. He makes it possible for straggly branches to produce delicious fruit that will demonstrate the beauty of the Lord our God.

The Lord Jesus said that His Father would fulfill the role of Vinedresser. He has full responsibility for keeping the branches pruned so that they become increasingly fruitful and for removing those branches which fail to bring forth fruit (John 15:1-2). The disciple of Jesus Christ needs to be continually aware of the glory of being a branch of the true Vine and never to forget that the Vinedresser still wields His knife for the good of the Vine and the increasing of spiritual productivity.

In a sense, this was what Jehovah was doing to Israel. As the Vinedresser, He was busy pruning, refining, and caring for the Vine He had chosen to bring forth His fruit.

We should remember that fruit is the outward evidence of the life inside. Grape life inside vines produces grapes outside the vines. God's life inside Israel should have produced godliness in Jerusalem. But even with the life of God clearly in the laws He had taught and in His glorious presence in the temple, the branches had failed.

Contemporary Christians are susceptible to the same failure. With all the evidences of the presence of the Lord in the fellowship of believers, the communion of saints, the ministry of the Word, the gifts of the Spirit, there can be a barrenness that belies the life. There may even be a wildness and a "sour-grapes" bitterness that contradicts the life. This will not be allowed to persist by the Vinedresser. Ezekiel still speaks today.

Poor Little Rich Girl

It seems as if the momentum of Ezekiel's ministry was building up. The words he spoke were becoming more and more challenging and at times downright offensive to his listeners. None more so than Ezekiel's parable of the poor little rich girl.

A baby girl was abandoned in a field on the day of her birth. None of the usual things had been done for the baby. Her umbilical cord was uncut; her body had not been washed or cleansed with salt; no "swaddling clothes" had been given to her. She was a piteous sight, but because of her mixed parentage and her unpleasant appearance, no one showed compassion to her.

Along came a stranger who, seeing the abandoned child, took care of the situation and commanded that the child dying in her own blood should live. Provision was made for her so that she grew to be a beautiful, charming, and poised young lady. Thanks, of course, to the benevolent stranger.

Years later, he returned to the neighborhood, saw the beautiful girl whom he had rescued and cared for, fell in love with her, and proposed marriage. She accepted and they were married, presumably to live happily ever after.

But they didn't because the girl, for reasons known only to herself, accepted the clothes and the jewels, the status and the prosperity of her loving husband, but never accepted him. She took all she could get but never gave herself. She became increasingly arrogant and selfish, and eventually, shamelessly and openly had affairs with other men. She introduced her children to her lifestyle, used her husband's home and goods to further her own unfaithfulness, and even went into business establishing centers of immorality around the neighborhood.

Hers was a story of abject shame, dishonor, and unspeakable ingratitude. Accustomed as they were to storytellers and storytelling, the inhabitants of Tel-abib loved this kind of tale. But the application of the story raised not a few eyebrows and maybe even a few fists!

Ezekiel's point was that Israel was the ugly, unwanted child of mixed parentage, lying in the field among the nations, disregarded and despised. The Lord had come and rescued her for no other reason that it is His nature to pity the pitiable and rescue the lost. He had cared for and loved the despised people, marrying them to Himself and setting His eternal purposes upon them. He had blessed them among the nations, shown His mighty power on their behalf, enriched them, and given them the tools to show forth His glory among the nations. But they had used their status to promote their own sin. They had abused their blessings and used them to their own willful ends, and generally had brought unspeakable shame to their heavenly Husband. (See Ezek. 16: 1-34).

Through Ezekiel, the Lord announced that He would deal with Israel in the manner of an abused husband. Publicly disgraced by His wife, He would publicly disgrace her before the ones with whom she had misbehaved.

To add weight to His words, the Lord reminded His "wife" of her two sisters, Sodom and Samaria, whom she despised. "They didn't do half the things you did, but I dealt with them. So don't think for a minute that I will fail to deal with you," He said. "Sodom was truly guilty of all manner of things, but not like you. Her problem was that she became self-satisfied and selfish, caring nothing for those in need around her. She became lazy and thoroughly obnoxious, wallowing in luxury while those around her struggled with insurmountable problems. To a certain degree, the same was true of Samaria. You thought you were far superior to both of your sisters, but you were far worse. I judged them; and I will judge you" (see 16:35-59).

A note of impending judgment sounded from the Lord's prophet, but remember that there was always a message of hope, a promise of something better. "I will bring back your sisters from their captivity and restore them to their rightful place, and when they return you will return too" (see 16:60-63).

The Covenant

Charles Lee Feinberg, commenting on Ezekiel's presentation of God's dealings with His "unfaithful wife" Israel wrote in *The Prophecy of Ezekiel,* "God can no more help being gracious than He can cease being God. He is the God of all grace, and He always finds a covenant basis on which He can exercise His grace." This is beautifully true of God's ways with His people. Ezekiel quoted the Lord's words, "Nevertheless, I will remember My covenant with thee in the days of thy youth and I will establish unto thee an everlasting covenant" (16:60). At the very time that He was pronouncing His judgments, the Lord was announcing His covenant.

Such statements seem so contradictory to us that some commentators believe that the sections dealing with eternal covenants in the context of judgment are obviously in the wrong place and probably belong in another part of the prophecy. Without denying the possibility that some parts of the manuscript were shuffled over the years, it hardly seems necessary to suggest that the Lord could not speak in grace at the same time He spoke in judgment. Surely this is the essence of Calvary, where grace and justice met and "righteousness and peace kissed each other."

The everlasting covenant God announced to His people was designed, as we have come to expect, to let the people know that He is the Lord. He is Lord not only of unfailing mercy, but One willing to take the most unfaithful and restore them to positions of trust and opportunity. He was willing to take Israel and make her a blessing to the nations of the world.

The same God has shown that He was willing to take murderer Moses and make him a leader of men; adulterer David and through him bring sinners to repentance; persecutor Saul and make him Paul, the missionary par excellence; and slave trader John Newton and make him a minister of the Gospel. It has been demonstrated through the years that the everlasting covenant of our God is one of forgiveness and unbelievable trust. He is prepared to run the risk of placing irresponsible and unfaithful people in areas of responsibility. He gives second chances to the repentant and superb opportunities to the undeserving. He is eternally committed to being a forgiving and restoring God.

What a humbling thing for the forgiven and the restored to realize. Ezekiel said that those so forgiven would "remember and be confounded and never open their mouths again" (16:63). I'm sure he didn't mean to contradict the psalmist who insisted that the "redeemed of the Lord" should "say so" (Ps. 107:2). Rather, they should never open their mouths to brag and boast again but only to proclaim "the riches of the glory of His grace."

Bold Eagle

Still another parable or riddle came from the Tel-abib storyteller's lips. He described a large eagle with beautiful plumage flying into the branches of a cedar of Lebanon and cropping off the highest branch. Then the eagle flew with it to an interesting place described as "a land of traffic" and a "city of merchants." At the same time, he picked up some seed from the land and planted it in a fertile place where the seed grew into a "spreading vine of low stature" (17:1-6).

Then along came another eagle and the vine began to turn its branches away from the first eagle to the second. The idea was, of course, that the vine thought a better deal could be gained from the second eagle (17:7-8).

The Lord has definite views on this kind of opportunism, and asked whether the vine should be allowed to survive this kind of behavior. His implication was that the vine would not, but rather must expect to be uprooted and wither (17:9-10).

To prevent any misunderstanding of the "riddle" and misinterpretation of the truth contained in it, God explained.

As we might expect, the vine was Israel and the "top branch" that was carried away referred to the cream of the crop carried into captivity by King Nebuchadnezzar of Babylon. At the same time, the Babylonian had shown considerable restraint in setting

Zedekiah on the throne in a puppet role on the basis of an "oath" taken by Zedekiah before the Lord. The arrangement was that a kind of mutual toleration would operate and there was a real possibility that if the oath was kept, peace and prosperity would reign (17:12-14).

However, Zedekiah got the idea that since Egypt, the second eagle, was quite a military power, it would probably make a good ally and might be the means of overthrowing the Babylonians. Both Ezekiel and Jeremiah were opposed to this idea for two reasons. First, it would entail the breaking of the oath Zedekiah had made. Second, the people of Israel should not be allowed to think that they could avert the judgment of God through political maneuvering and treachery. In fact, this would only bring more wrath upon them (17:15-21).

Zedekiah refused to listen and went ahead with his scheming and conniving. Ezekiel predicted that his ill-timed, ill-conceived ideas would lead to further disaster. Shortly after this prophecy his words were confirmed and the city of Jerusalem was overthrown and the people decimated (17:20-21).

Integrity

It is fascinating to note that while the Lord had no special affection for the Babylonians, He was prepared to use them to further His purposes with His own people. Nor should we overlook the fact that the Lord regarded the treaty that Zedekiah had made with Nebuchadnezzar as involving Him. He called it "My oath" and "My covenant" (17:19), even though it was made with an unbelieving nation.

Evidently the Lord takes it very seriously when His people enter into any kind of contractual agreement. His own integrity is at stake if those who name His name show a lack of this trait. Even when contracts and covenants are made with those who are not the Lord's, the contract involves Him.

Surely a nation with any kind of godly heritage and which uses His name should have a high standard of political integrity, both domestically and internationally. Even when dealing with nations that have no such integrity, whose principles and policies are completely the opposite.

Surely when those who know the Lord sign a union contract, a high standard of commitment is to be expected from them, if for no other reason than that they bring with their signature a sense of divine integrity.

But perhaps the area in which we most need a high commitment to integrity is in marriage. I am tired and disgusted with the innumerable excuses voiced by those who "want out" of their marital contracts. Believers need to be told that when they made a contract in this holy and precious area of human experience, the contract in a special way involved the Lord. It is a contract related to His institution, presided over by one who stands there as His servant, performed in a place known as His house, and sealed with His benediction.

Christian contractors, beware! In the eyes of God there is no place for the broken contract, as Zedekiah and his people discovered to their sorrow.

In this series of parables and riddles, allegories and pantomimes, Ezekiel covered a lot of ground. His hearers and watchers had seen and heard a lot, but it was still questionable how much they had *really* seen and heard. But the earnest and the reverent among them had understood. This has always been the case: those who carefully hear and consider the Word of God can count on the Lord to give them understanding.

Today the Church must look at God's dealings with Israel and learn the lessons of the fruitless vine and the unfaithful wife. She must beware of the temptation to build a whitewashed partition and see the danger of the second eagle. The Lord means business and has every intention of working among His people to make them increasingly conversant with Him and His demands so that He can let the world know that He is the Lord.

8

The Loud Silence of God

Ezekiel 18—20

"Passing the buck" is all too common. Recently our dishwasher rusted through while still under guarantee. A clear-cut case of inferior workmanship and shoddy materials. But you wouldn't believe the hassle we got into with the dealership. "It must be your water." "What kind of detergents did you use?" "We need to come over and look at it, and our fee for sending a man is $25.00."

Of course, there's nothing new about "buck-passing." When Adam found himself cornered by God in the garden after he had eaten the forbidden fruit, he explained the tragedy by passing the buck to "the woman whom thou gavest to be with me" (Gen. 3:12). I'm not sure if Adam was blaming God or Eve, but I don't think he minded who got blamed just so long as he didn't. Eve, however, wasn't having any of that. She passed the buck to the serpent who she said "beguiled me" (3:13).

The contemporary philosophy called "determinism" theorizes that all events, including moral choices, are predetermined by events and situations that preclude the possibility of man acting freely or independently of those events or situations. If someone is born in a ghetto or is a member of a broken family with a brother who is a convicted thief, he can hardly be blamed for getting into a life of crime.

There is no doubt that environment and heredity and circumstances greatly influence the development of personality and per-

THE LOUD SILENCE OF GOD / 91

formance, but to lay everything at the feet of society and refuse
to accept personal responsibility is grossly out of order and ultimately totally destructive. This is passing the buck too far! What
man will feel like a man and try to live like a man if he believes
that he bears no responsibility for his actions and must settle for
living his life as a victim of circumstances determined before he
was born? It is far better to tell him that each person has an individual responsibility before God, whatever his circumstances and
formative experiences. Ezekiel had to tell the people of the Tel
exactly that.

Sour Grapes
One day the people gathered outside Ezekiel's house and, in response to his message from the Lord, quoted a well-known
proverb: "The fathers have eaten sour grapes, and the children's
teeth are set on edge" (18:2).

The Lord reacted strongly to this and told Ezekiel to ban the
proverb. "Tell the people that as surely as I am alive, Ezekiel,
they will no longer be allowed to quote this proverb" (18:3). The
reason was apparent. The people of the Exile were saying that it
was their parents who had rebelled against God and that they are
suffering for their parents' rebellion. The previous generation had
eaten the grapes, but the younger generation was tasting the sour-
ness. They had decided there was nothing they could do about
anything, and therefore they might as well settle down into a kind
of fatalism and live a life of total irresponsibility.

Added to this attitude of despair and hopelessness mixed with
a kind of disgruntled resignation, was something extremely serious.
They were not only passing the buck to their parents but also trying to pass it on to God. They were proclaiming loud and clear,
"The way of the Lord is not just. How can He be just when He
judges us for the things our parents did?" To this the Lord responded through His long-suffering servant.

Third and Fourth Generations
Before we get into a consideration of the Lord's reply to the
charge that He was not just, let us remind ourselves of the circumstances behind the reasoning of the younger generation. The
Lord had certainly taught that He would "visit the iniquity of the
fathers upon the children unto the third and fourth generation"

(Ex. 20:5; Num. 14:18), an apparently grossly inequitable state of affairs.

However, study of these Scriptures makes clear that God does not judge one person for another's sin, but if sons indulge in their father's sins unto the third and fourth generation, God will judge each generation. In this case, God goes on judging generation after generation on the basis of each one bearing his own guilt and condemnation.

There is another sense in which God visits the sins of fathers on the children. In the economy of God, causes produce effects and sin is no exception. We are familiar with the situation in which a young boy who has been greatly mistreated by his father has severe psychological disturbances that lead him to antisocial behavior. Or the case of the unfaithful wife and mother who so disrupts the family by her selfishness and waywardness that the kids run away from home and end up in a prison cell.

On a much larger scale, we are familiar with sins of a societal nature which have resulted in a society's upheaval generations after the event. I believe that many black and white kids who are being shipped from one end of town to another where they are neither appreciated nor wanted are suffering because of the gross abuse of the black people by our white forefathers. The sins of slavery are still showing their bitter fruits upon contemporary American society.

While there is a sense in which society's sins affect the innocent, and previous generations' crimes bring forth fruit decades later, the fact remains that every individual is responsible for his own sin. He may suffer innocently or be the victim of unavoidable circumstances, but that will never alter the fact of his responsibility. How can anything alter the fact that all have sinned and are morally responsible?

Like Father, Like Son

Personal responsibility was the point the Lord began to enunciate through Ezekiel. "Behold all souls are mine; as the soul of the father, so also the soul of the son is mine: the soul that sinneth it shall die" (18:4). The statement is clear enough. God insists that every person stand before Him and answer to Him for what he has or has not done.

Such a message must have been earthshaking to the people of

Tel-abib. Though conscious of their special standing as a nation before God, and aware that their national destiny was wrapped up in their relationship to God, they had fallen into the trap of thinking that sin was something vaguely social and national and its ramifications would be social and national too. They were right to a certain extent, but they did not recognize the fact that national sin is the accumulation of personal sin, and societal guilt is the product of individual rebellion. True, there were national and social sins with national and social consequences, yet the exiles needed to face the unpleasant fact that they were the ones sinning and that they would be the ones experiencing the judgment of God.

There is something strangely comforting in the idea that society is wrong, not me, and therefore, society will be judged, not me. But God was telling the people of the Exile that society was wrong because they were wrong and their society would be judged as they were judged.

To stress the point that people are individually responsible and that iniquity and righteousness do not run in the bloodstream, the Lord gave the example of three men—a grandfather, his son, and grandson (see 18:5-20). Some commentators see in the illustration a reference to Hezekiah, Manasseh, and Josiah, three of Judah's kings who would fit the description.

If the grandfather lives a just life by doing what is lawful and right, his righteousness will not be credited to his son who does all manner of evil. In the same way, if the grandson does what is lawful and right, neither the righteousness of his grandfather nor the sinfulness of his father will have any bearing on his situation. Only his own righteousness will be revelant.

It is interesting to note the details of the "just" life which were given to the people by Ezekiel. They included separation from anything that savored of idolatry, sexual purity in marital and premarital relationships, meticulous fairness in financial and business dealings, a deep involvement in ministry to the underprivileged, and a readiness to be involved in the resolution of societal problems (18:6-8, 15-17).

The Just and the Unjust

We need to be reminded that the Lord was promising life to those who were just, and death to those who were unjust. It is easy to see how one could gain the impression from such Scriptures as these that a man can be justified by his works. Yet the clear teaching of the New Testament flatly denies this concept and makes the strong statement that man is "justified by faith without the deeds of the law" (Rom. 3:28).

The reason for the difficulty is that we interpret the terms used in the Old Testament from a New Testament vantage point and invest the terms of the Old with the insights of the New. For instance, the just man to whom Ezekiel refers is not the man "justified by faith" of whom Paul spoke. Paul himself pointed out that he would have qualified as a just man by Ezekiel's definition because he was blameless when it came to "righteousness which is in the law" (Phil. 3:6). The righteousness which came from being a law-abiding Jew, however, was quite different from the righteousness that comes freely from God through grace. It would be possible for an Israelite to do all the right things and never do any of the wrong things, but to have the wrong motives for his actions. He would be outwardly just but inwardly unjust. He needed to have a heart that was right before God as well as a life that was right before men. This "right heart" could come only through the forgiveness of God offered freely by His grace and received gratefully by faith.

Similar things could be said about the terms "life" and "death." With the advantage of New Testament truth behind us, we immediately think of "eternal life" and "eternal separation from God" when we hear the terms "life" and "death," but it was not quite so clear to Ezekiel and his contemporaries. Their concepts of life and death were very closely tied into earthly life and physical death, and their ideas of fullness of life and the barrenness of death were tied into their concepts of dying in the wilderness and living peacefully in the Promised Land. Let us not forget, however, that the principles are the same for New Testament oriented people. Individuals who are outwardly just cannot pass on their righteousness to their progeny any more than rascals automatically procure condemnation for their children. Each person stands before God, and in the fullest sense the "soul that sinneth it shall die" (Ezek. 18:20).

New Hearts for Old
The emphasis on the individual was stressed even further as

Ezekiel warmed to his theme. He began to make an appeal to individuals to become rightly related to God. In the same way that their individual sin had led them to individual judgment, so their individual repentance would lead them to individual forgiveness. In fact, the Lord made clear through His servant that contrary to what some people seemed to think, He had "no pleasure in the death of him that dieth" (18:32). He urged the people therefore to come to the point of making individual commitments and responses to the Lord. "Make you a new heart and a new spirit, for why will ye die?" He said (18:31) Before we get overly excited about the "make you" let us remember that Ezekiel had said that the Lord had promised a new heart and a new spirit (11:19). There is no contradiction in these statements, just two sides to the same transaction.

It's not unlike the two-sided statement in Philippians 2:12-13: "Work out your own salvation with fear and trembling. For it is God which worketh in you both to will and to do of His good pleasure." There is the human and divine aspect in all human-divine experiences. We are totally locked into the necessity of God working in us and giving us a new heart and spirit, yet this cannot happen unless we cooperate by "making a new heart" and "working out." In other words, when God sees that we are earnest, He moves in power.

Mother Lion and Cubs

Ezekiel's remarkable versatility was demonstrated by his next action. He sat down and composed a lamentation, or a dirge. A lamentation was a special poem with a particularly mournful rhythm. Jeremiah was a master of the lamentation, but other writers used it too. For instance, David's psalms show his familiarity with the device.

Ezekiel's poem is simply to understand. Israel, pictured as a lioness, has mothered some fine young "lions" or "princes." The first one was trapped by the Egyptians—a reference to Jehoahaz who was captured by Pharaoh Necho. Mother Lion went back to her cubs and raised another prince but he fell prey to the Babylonians—a reference to Jehoiachin (see Ezek. 19:2-9).

The last part of the dirge moved away from the picture of the lioness and her cubs to the theme of the vine. Mother Lion became Mother Vine, a beautiful example of artistic license, not to mention mixed metaphor! No matter, the end result was the same. The vine was uprooted and instead of bringing forth the "rod" that would rule, she languished in the desert and was finally destroyed (19:10-12). The appalling result of all this was that "she hath no strong rod to be a scepter to rule" (19:14).

Israel, whether a lion or a vine, had produced a succession of leaders who had fallen prey to the nations around them. This was judgment of God, and the end was in sight.

Here Come the Elders

One day after he had sung his dirge to the assembled watchers and listeners, Ezekiel received a delegation of elders. They came to see if he had any more words from the Lord. They sat down before Ezekiel and waited to see if the Lord would communicate anything to them through His servant. Perhaps they anticipated a long wait like the one they had had on a previous visit when Ezekiel was "transported" to Jerusalem. We don't know what they expected, but they probably weren't expecting what they received.

The Lord quickly let Ezekiel know what He had to say in response to the inquiry of the elders. "Tell them that they have an awful nerve coming to inquire of Me, Ezekiel. I have spoken to them continuously and they have not heard Me so I have nothing further to say to them. I will not be inquired of by them" (see Ezek. 20:3).

It must have been hard for Ezekiel to tell the elders what the Lord wanted him to say. Imagine his saying to them, "The Lord says He has said all He's going to say to you."

"But why? Why won't He respond to us? Surely He has always been ready to hear, Ezekiel. There must be some mistake."

"The Lord says He will not speak to you because all through the history of your people, He has spoken and what He has said has been disregarded so He has nothing more to say."

Silence

The silence of God is perhaps more frightening than the Word of God. To be confronted with God's Word may be unnerving and challenging, but to be told that He has nothing more to say must be terrifying.

Pontius Pilate experienced the silence of the Lord Jesus. When he asked where the Lord came from, he got no answer because He had made it perfectly clear that He came from the Father. Pilate wouldn't accept that so He kept trying to get a different answer until in the end, he asked one time too many and got only silence. (See John 18:33—19:9.)

Herod was excited about meeting Jesus, not because he believed that He was who He claimed to be, but because he was always glad to meet a celebrity. So he plied Jesus with one question after another and never got a single answer (Luke 23:8-9). The Lord wasn't about to waste His breath entertaining someone who needed something much more than entertainment.

There is a solemn truth to be learned from the elders of Tel-abib and the men who met the Lord Jesus in the final days of His earthly ministry. It is that God reserves the right to talk as long as He wishes and to be silent when He has said enough. Perhaps to modern ears, the silence of God is a strange sound, startling in its impact because they have not learned that to ply God with questions and subjects for discussion is an exercise in futility when He decides He has had enough.

So that there would be no misunderstanding, the Lord instructed Ezekiel to explain why He had no interest in further debate and discussion with the elders. "Give them a brief review of the history of Israel, Ezekiel, and show them that I have been talking to them for centuries but they have not obeyed Me" (Ezek. 20:5).

At this point Ezekiel's approach changed dramatically. He laid aside his metaphors and dirges, his drama and his songs, and gave them a straightforward history lesson.

The History Lesson

History is not everyone's favorite subject, but it is important nevertheless, particularly to the Jew and the Christian. John Bright in his book, *The Authority of the Old Testament* (SCM Press, 1967, p. 77) called Israel's history "the theatre of God's purposive activity." He intended to show that anyone reading the story of the experiences of the people of Israel would be reading the special story of a special people in whose midst God was especially at work revealing Himself. This is of the greatest importance to us who live centuries after the events took place. If it can be ascertained that the events actually occurred, then it should not be too difficult for even the most timid soul to believe not only that "God is" but also to see in the biblical revelation what *sort* of God He is.

Archaeologists have been doing sterling work in recent years, and their findings have consistently verified the history recorded in the Old Testament. The reverent soul may not be particularly interested in having the Old Testament documents verified as far as their historical accuracy is concerned, but many not so reverent and slightly more questioning souls are being confronted with evidence which must lead them to see the truthfulness of the Old Testament as history and the true revelation of God in that history. Moreover, as Christians study the verifiable history of the people of Israel, they see a glorious picture of "the God and Father of our Lord Jesus Christ" at work.

Danger! God at Work

Ezekiel's summary was brief and pertinent. God had chosen Israel and made Himself known to them in the land of Egypt. He introduced Himself to them with the words, "I am the Lord your God." After taking this initiative, He committed Himself to "bring them forth of the land of Egypt into a land . . . flowing with milk and honey" which He said was "the glory of all lands" (Ezek. 20:5-6).

The call, the Exodus, and the Hebrews' entrance into Canaan are historical facts. Ezekiel knew it, the elders knew it, and we know it too. But the important thing to remember about these facts is that they reveal God at work, calling, delivering, and providing for His children in a superlative manner.

There was, however, a large fly in the ointment. The Lord insisted that the children of Israel leave their idols behind. They refused, but He was patient with them. He took them into the wilderness, and gave them His laws and judgments, and insisted that they observe the Sabbath. They were to be a unique people in the midst of the other nations, doing such weird things as turning from idols, worshiping one God, taking time off when others were working, and all sorts of other things that would make the pagans around them sit up and take notice. But they wouldn't keep the statutes, they despised the judgments, and messed around with the Sabbaths, so they were just like the people around them.

It was the Lord's intention to deal forcibly with His recalcitrant children, but He determined to give them another chance in the wilderness. He allowed one generation of rebels to pass away and gave an opportunity for their sons and daughters to learn from the mistakes of their parents and follow the Lord. The ironic thing about the instructions God gave to His people was that they were designed for the well-being of the people. But the Israelites thought they were missing something by going the route that God laid before them, and they were right! They were going to miss the kind of life He promises to those who obey Him.

The more I minister among people, the more I am struck by the disintegration of life that follows disobedience to God and by the amazing content to be found in the life of those who follow Him. The observation of moral, ethical, physical, and social principles as laid down in Scripture does ensure a wholeness of life, and the neglect of them leads to all manner of individual and social disintegration.

The second generation Israelites were no better than the first. This posed a massive problem for the Lord because He had brought His children out of Egypt to install them in Canaan. The pagan nations were watching this remarkable maneuver with bated breath. They were witnessing the biggest demonstration of divine power imaginable. If God refused to take His people into the Promised Land, His own Name would be besmirched among the pagans and His objective would have been thwarted. Yet He was long-suffering with His uncooperative people and led them into the land of Canaan but with very strict instructions and promises.

Molech

The minute they arrived in Canaan, God's people headed for the pagan shrines and took off after the pagan deities in open rejection of the Lord's requirements. He told them that they would be scattered among the pagan nations; He also told them something that is a little hard to understand. He said, "I polluted them with their own gifts in that they caused to pass through the fire all that openeth the womb" (20:26).

There is no unanimity among scholars as to the exact meaning of this statement. We would be safe in assuming, however, that the Lord decided to allow the children of Israel to do what they wanted to do, even to the point of offering as sacrifices to Molech their firstborn, who belonged to the Lord. God wanted the people who were intent on sinning to go to whatever point was necessary to discover the extreme sinfulness of their actions.

I believe God acts through the experiences of the sin, even though its results are appalling. It ought not to be too difficult for us to see why God does this if we remember some of the things parents must do with their children who are intent on going their own way despite all warnings to the contrary.

My dad once told me about his one and only experience with smoking. When he was about 10, he decided to experiment with the weed. He came home from the experiment with the smell of it on his clothes.

His old grandmother had no difficulty recognizing the symptoms, so she said, "Stanley, I've been thinking that it's about time you started smoking. You're a young man now. Go down to the tobacconist's store and buy a clay pipe and an ounce of Black Twist. Then take a boat out on the lake and have a nice relaxing afternoon."

He couldn't believe his good fortune! Imagine such luck! What he didn't know was that Black Twist was the most potent tobacco available and that even veteran smokers wouldn't use a new clay pipe without first breaking it in gradually. And smoking it in a gently rocking boat!

Well, the end of the story was not quite so idyllic as the beginning and it may be tempting to say, "What a wretch of a woman that grandmother was. To do a thing like that to a 10-year-old is unthinkable." My dad didn't talk like that. He learned that she had acted in love by allowing him to go the way he was going to go. But by exaggerating the consequences of his action, she managed to save him from a habit that would have proved extremely detrimental to him over the years.

Incidentally, her action was so successful that it spilled over to me and to both my sons! Sounds like something to third and fourth generations!

To Whom Much Is Given
While we have been talking about Black Twist, the elders have been sitting in Ezekiel's counseling room. Ezekiel was concluding his history lesson. He had shown how God had acted in the history of the Israelites and how they had repeatedly overridden every-

thing He had said or done. At this point Ezekiel brought his history right up-to-date and said to the elders, "Are you polluted like your fathers were? How dare you sit there and say to yourselves, 'We will be like the heathen, worshiping stone and wood as the people of the nations do' " (See 20:30, 32).

His statement was a blunt exposé of what was going on in the hearts of the elders even as they sat before the prophet purporting to "inquire of the Lord." They were actually unrepentant about their own idolatry, set in their ways despite the exile, and committed to an external form of Jehovah worship while maintaining in their hearts an affinity with what the Lord had condemned throughout their long, long history.

In God's eyes, they were not as bad as the people in the wilderness—they were worse. They had the advantage of history. They had the prophets. They had received accumulated revelations, and the more they had received, the more God expected of them. "To whom much is given shall much be required" (see Luke 12:48). But instead of learning from history and heeding the prophets, they had gone ahead with their sin and were still going ahead with it even as they said they were inquiring of the Lord.

Nothing to Say

God finally put His foot down and said, "I will not be inquired of by you." The elders met the silence of God.

Before we get too condemnatory about them, let's remind ourselves that from the vantage point of history we have far more to go on than they ever had. We have the knowledge of Christ, the beauty of His life, the glory of His cross, the triumph of His resurrection, and the wonder of His ascension and intercession at the right hand of the Father. This they did not know, but we do.

Applying the principles of God's dealings with the Israelites to ourselves, could it be that our present moral, ethical, psychological, sociological, economical, and political situation is the product of God allowing us to smoke Black Twist in a rocking boat? Could it be that we are going ahead with our idolatry despite all these evidences of disintegration, while at the same time we maintain a posture of religious rectitude and pious integrity?

We inquire of the Lord but have not learned that He has chosen to keep His silence. I believe that for many individuals the silence of God is a reality and will remain with them till they come to repentance, rid themselves of their idols, and walk distinctively before Him. The same can be said of some societies in our world at the present time.

Something to Say

One thing amazes me more than any other: The long-suffering of God. In the history lesson we just audited this was clearly shown. Having flatly told the elders that they would not hear from Him, however, the Lord told them that in the same way that their forebears had suffered the wilderness because of their resistance, they would suffer another wilderness called the Exile. But as He had promised the land to the wilderness people, He would promise a return to the land for the exiles (20:33-41). Even at the moment of tough talking, the Lord speaks a loving promise. When He is being driven to the point of exasperation, He outlines to them the plans He has for them. That's love, patience, and long-suffering! That is the God of history!

This promise of restoration should have been sweet to the taste of the elders, but it is unlikely they even heard what He was saying. They loved their sin with its awful consequences more than the service of the living God with all its beautiful advantages. Nevertheless, Ezekiel ploughed ahead with his message.

Perhaps you think God is being contradictory because on the one hand He is saying "I will not be inquired of by you," yet He keeps on talking. We talk about the silence of God, but it's pretty loud silence!

We should understand that God was perfectly prepared to talk to them about the things they needed to hear. It was just that He was not about to engage in conversation concerning things that were immaterial. They probably wanted to talk about restoration to the land while He wanted to talk about idolatry. Their interests were mainly in the area of their own advantage; His were in the field of His own glory. On the top of their agenda was, "How can we get what we want?" The sole item on His agenda was, "What do I have to do to bring My people to Myself?" They had gone round and round on these subjects without getting anywhere, so God had finally decided to adjourn the conference until the elders would listen to Him.

I firmly believe this is a warning to the Church of today. Our agendas are full of brilliant ideas, wonderful schemes, dazzling projects, astronomical budgets, and grandiose objectives, but His agenda has one basic item, "How can I bring the Church to the point of being the Church so that My schemes, objectives, and projects might be fulfilled in such a way that the pagans will look at the Church and say, 'The Living God is in their midst'?"

9

The Man in the Gap

Ezekiel 21—24

People react to hard truth in different ways. Some say, "That's too complicated for me to understand. Anyway, it's all a matter of interpretation and I have no training in that area. Even if I had, I probably wouldn't understand it because most of those guys who've been to seminary can't agree on what the Bible is saying. So I guess only God knows." Others try to make a joke out of the things that are serious. No doubt you have seen men kidding the pastor about something he preached or ribbing each other about their own lack of dedicated response to what has been taught them.

Ezekiel ran into similar problems. At one point in his ministry he complained, "Ah Lord God! They say of me, 'Doth he not speak parables?' " (20:49). John Taylor comments that the literal meaning of their words is "a riddler of riddles." I've heard preachers called many things, but that's a new one! In all fairness to Ezekiel's congregation, we must admit there was some justification for their comments. But Ezekiel was not such a "riddler" that honest open minds and hearts could not understand his basic message.

Sword of the Lord
When Ezekiel took up a sword one day, sharpened it, and then began a whirling sword dance, the people evidently thought it

quite amusing because he broke off in the middle and said to them, "Should we make mirth?" (21:10) The answer was obviously no when we bear in mind that he was illustrating the awfulness of the "sword of the Lord" being used against the people of Israel. For years they had enjoyed divine intervention on their behalf and had rejoiced in the sword being used against their enemies. In fact, they knew that without the sword they would have had no national identity or social survival. But to be told that the sword was now against them instead of for them was more than they were prepared to take. So they laughed at the messenger and ridiculed the methodology rather than face up to the message.

Perhaps it was these evasive tactics of the people that led the Lord to direct Ezekiel to make one of the clearest statements of his ministry. "Thus saith the Lord God, 'Remove the diadem and take off the crown. . . . I will overturn, overturn, overturn it; and he shall be no more until he come whose right it is; and I will give it to him" (21:26-27).

The triple "overturn" is not the result of a faulty typewriter but the strongest device in the Hebrew language for emphasizing a point. The ones who wore the symbols of majesty and honor were to be stripped of their honor and relieved of their position, and no one would take their place till the great King, the One who would reign in righteousness, made His appearance. It was a clear Messianic promise to the people who were taking the Word of God lightly.

Number One

Ezekiel went on, at the Lord's direction, to spell out the specifics of the situation and also to show something that He had not yet revealed. The Lord told the people He had been looking for a man to "stand in the gap" but had been unable to find one (22:30). The situation was hopeless.

The verse to which we have just referred is perhaps the most famous verse in the prophecy. I am convinced that it spells out something of great importance to the contemporary Church, namely, the inestimable value of "a man"—one person committed to serving the Lord. In our contemporary environment we think on a global scale, involve ourselves in mass enterprises, and generally subscribe to the theory that "might is right" and "bigger is better." But Scripture insists that the individual committed to the Lord is the factor that changes the world. In the numbers game the most important number is "one."

We can see this truth, which we may be overlooking, in a startling perspective when we bear in mind that the Lord was speaking about a national situation and a societal malady. The value of the individual is of such remarkable proportions that it can affect for good or evil a nation or a society.

The Lord went on, "Son of man, say unto her [the house of Israel], 'Thou art the land that is not cleansed nor rained upon in the day of indignation'" (22:24). Scholars have had a little problem with the word "cleansed." Some have suggested "showered" and others "shined upon." Whoever is right, the picture is clear: the land suffered from physical and spiritual drought and barrenness. The people were very conscious of their dependence on the water supply, for they had been told that an evidence of divine favor was plentiful water (Lev. 26:3-4). Divine disapproval would be shown by a lack of the showers and rain that would multiply their harvest. So they could not avoid the evidence of divine displeasure every time they went to the drying well or looked at the withering landscape.

Drought

It's interesting to note that many areas of the world are suffering from physical drought at the same time that many countries are spiritually withered. A dryness and a barrenness is abroad in our world and not least in the areas where traditionally and historically tangible blessings of God have been most evident. This should make us pause in thought, unless we have rationalized the situation to such an extent that we don't really think God involves Himself in meteorology or any other scientific project. I wouldn't be dogmatic about God and meteorology, but I do not hesitate to say that spiritual drought, both on a personal and a corporate level, is directly attributable to God withholding the flow of His blessing because of the stubbornness of His people.

Having made the blanket statement concerning the land, the Lord embarked on a complete analysis of the situation. I find this both fascinating and alarming. Fascinating, because I'm intrigued with the idea of God not only observing what is happening on His earth, but also evaluating what is happening and analyzing the causes. Alarming, because I like to think of God being as general as possible. The more detailed He becomes, the more uncomfortable I begin to feel!

For instance, I suppose that all of us can live comfortably with the thought that God is deeply disturbed when He looks down from heaven and sees a city full of people lost in their sin. That is understandable and not too challenging. But what if God is going further than that and actually saying to Himself, "Why is that city so lost when I have put My people in that city? Let's take a look at First Baptist, First Presbyterian, St. Mark's Episcopal, and Calvary Assembly of God for a start and evaluate what they are doing. It may be that the lostness of the city is directly related to the condition of My people." Then it gets tough!

Getting Specific

It seems quite clear to me that God directed Ezekiel to explain to the exiles that the general condition of the land was directly related to the condition of specific groups of people. He also insisted that this be made known. First He talked about the prophets (22:25), then the priests (22:26), and then the politicians (22:27), the prophets again (22:28), and finally the people (22:29). A list which covered every echelon of society.

It is important for us to remember that at the time the nation's government was a theocracy. True, God had grudgingly given into the demand of His people that they have a monarchy like the nations round about them. This moved them from the special, unique system He wanted for them. Nevertheless, He was involved in the affairs of the nation and insisted that His principles be practiced by everyone, regardless of social strata. He was prepared to allow them a theocratic monarchy if they insisted on having a king. This is almost incomprehensible to us, governed as we are by democratic thoughts and secular considerations. We don't expect God to be God in every echelon of our society—but God expected it in Israel's society.

Princes

The Lord's evaluation of the "princes," that is, the royal household, was that they had "ripped off" the people both financially and spiritually (22:27). They had coldly and callously taken the people's land, destroyed their spiritual sensitivity, sent them to war, and generally brought havoc to their lives. The princes had grossly abused their power. Instead of leading the people in the way of the Lord for the good of the society and the glory of God, they had used their God-given authority to feather their own nests. In so doing, they had produced a shambles.

Priests

Turning His attention to the "priests" (22:26), the Lord was no less scathing in His denunciations. As a class of people, they had been guilty of violating the law they were expected to support. In addition, the Lord charged them with bringing into disrepute things He held dear. Through their own lack of commitment to the Lord, they had failed to draw careful distinctions between right and wrong. They had blurred the lines God had drawn and generally toned down the principles they had been called to uphold.

One of the classic illustrations of this was their neglect of the Sabbath. This may not seem very serious to us because our understanding of the Lord's Day is rather fuzzy. To the Lord, however, Sabbath-keeping was a matter of utmost importance, for it was one of the most distinctive features of the cultural life of His people. A distinction that He had instituted and insisted upon as a mark of their belonging to Him.

Politicians

The "politicians" were the next ones to be analyzed and exposed by the Lord (26:27). Strictly speaking, they were the men in positions of authority over families and larger groups of people but in subordinate roles to the princes, who headed God's list. Like the princes, the politicians were guilty of disregarding the people whom they were supposed to be leading.

Prophets

Then it was the turn of the "prophets" (26:28). Nobody would ever pretend that the role of prophet was designed to produce popularity. If we might paraphrase Gilbert and Sullivan, "A prophet's life was not a happy one, happy one!" By definition, prophets were required to "hear the Word of the Lord" and then go to the people and address them with statements prefaced by "thus saith the Lord." Unfortunately for the prophet, many of the Lord's words were critical of the status quo and opposed to the common wisdom. So there was a real temptation for the prophet to tone down his message or back off.

The prophets in Ezekiel's time were engaged in such weak preaching and teaching that the Lord charged them with doing a whitewash job at best, and being guilty of outright falsification at the worst. The seriousness of this situation becomes apparent when we remember how important it is for society to know what God says as well as what society thinks. If the prophetic voice is silenced, the people are locked into a solitary voice without any corrective note or divine perspective. It is bad enough if the prophetic voice is silenced, but when the messenger continues to talk but speaks less than God's Word or even contradicts God's Word while insisting that he is proclaiming the truth, unbelievable confusion is the result. The charge that the prophets were saying "thus saith the Lord God" when the Lord had not spoken is surely one of the most heinous of crimes before God and against humanity.

The People
The Lord then turned His attention to the common people who He said were guilty of all kinds of abuse. Perhaps they themselves had been gravely abused. While princes, politicians, prophets, and priests had all played their part in confusing, using, and abusing the people, the people had found other people they could abuse.

There was evidently a "pecking order" in Israelite society and woe betide the ones on the bottom of the order. Those who were being abused by the authorities were busy trying to get what they could from those less fortunate than themselves. I am reminded of the less than immortal words of the distinguished English mathematician Augustus de Morgan who wrote,

Great fleas have little fleas upon their
    backs to bite 'em,
And little fleas have lesser fleas and so
    ad infinitum.

Slag Heap
Starting at the top and working down to the bottom echelons of society, Israel's practices were a sad, bitter story of materialistic selfishness, greed, graft, indifference to suffering, and total

neglect of divine requirement. In short, its society had come apart at the seams.

Social disintegration is the inevitable result of corrupt leadership. The Lord was so disgusted by this state of affairs that He called the house of Israel "dross" and told them He would put them in a furnace of affliction to prove His point (22:18-22). The Old Testament often talked about the refining of metals as a picture of God's dealings with His people, but here God was saying that He didn't expect any metal to come out of the trial, only dross. They were, in His eyes, a slag heap!

Ezekiel outlined the details of this societal breakdown. He told the people that they "set light by father and mother" (22:7) meaning that discipline in the home was lacking. Parents were not taking their father and mother roles seriously, so naturally the kids weren't either. The predictable result was a total breakdown of any concept of discipline, social responsibility, or healthy relationships. Generations were being produced that knew nothing of the fundamentals of living with others.

If mothers and fathers don't teach their children early that they are not the only pebbles on the beach, the kids grow up believing that they are the only pebble and that the rest of the beach exists for their benefit. It would be tolerable if only one child felt this way. When a generation of young people refuses to accept the basic fact of many pebbles, however, everybody grows up intent on living only for himself, regardless of the damage done to others. These people live unhindered by such considerations as self-control and discipline.

Sex Drive

Ezekiel pointed out that undisciplined living leads to, among other things, all manner of sexual license (22:9-11). There is no denying the fact that God in His wisdom placed in His children a phenomenal motivating factor called the sex drive. As everybody knows, this sex drive has to be braked or it will run everybody over the cliff. But what brakes to use, when to use them, and who should apply them have been debated over the years.

These questions persist, of course, unless people have taken the simple expedient of checking with the Inventor of the sex drive. He gave instructions on how to steer, brake, and enjoy the sex drive. But the problem with this approach is that knowledge of His principles is necessary, submission to them is mandatory, and self-control is imperative.

Now if kids are raised in an environment where His rules are ignored at best and derided at worst, trouble looms. Coupled with this situation is the frightening possibility that those who have never been taught discipline will be strangers to self-control. The result will be a runaway trip motivated by an uncontrolled sex drive.

The trouble with an uncontrolled sex drive is boredom, and the answer to boredom is variety. God's sex principles leave limited room for variety; the rejection of these principles leaves unlimited possibilities of "exciting" perversions such as incest, adultery, and even bestiality. The emotional, psychological, and societal damage resulting from such activities is rarely considered by those who reject the divine principles and operate on the basis of unbridled passions. But this damage eats at the heart of the family structure, eventually destroys the conscience of the ones involved, and adds to the sorry heap of spiritual and moral destitution.

Violence

Closely related to the lack of parental discipline and sexual control was the subject of violence (22:12). The callous indifference to the status and needs of individuals and the outright denial of God's evaluation of a person leaves the door wide open to all manner of violence and physical abuse. Added to the economic rape of some and the sexual abuse of others, violence was producing the desperate fear that leads to violent activity which sometimes has no other purpose than survival. A sick, sorry state of affairs. At the root of the whole problem, as the Lord reminded the people, was the fact they had "forgotten Me" (22:12). A spiritual problem was causing the multitude of other problems.

Moral Morass

The parallels to our current scene are numerous and obvious, yet I believe I must mention them. So at the risk of overkill, let me suggest some simple applications.

The breakdown of biblical leadership in government circles, family circles, church circles, and any other kinds of circles where leadership can reasonably be expected is alarming. This has led to all kinds of abuse, and people have become cynical of any institution or social structure that could or should produce reliable, respectable, realistic leadership.

Cynical disregard of the abiding nature of the marriage contract is rife in every area of society. Distrust of public officials is rampant from the lowest local level to the highest international level.

The challenging prophetic message unique to the Church of Jesus Christ has to a great extent been silenced by a smooth, soothing message to those who will stand in line to be smoothed and soothed. The priestly function of the average believer holding firm the law of the Lord has been desperately jeopardized by His disciples' casual approach to His standards of discipleship. So a clear, distinct voice and witness of divine dissent is sadly lacking. From pulpit and pew alike comes a hum of approval for and a vote of confidence in our society rather than a howl of dismay and a shout of dissent.

Lacking clear-sighted, highly motivated leadership, and missing the trumpet call of the church to a discipleship and reiteration of Christ's law of loving obedience, it is no wonder that the countries of the Western world are wallowing in a morass of their own making. Some groups are concerned about injustice, violence, pornography, and crime, but their best efforts seem to be devoted to fighting it and banning it, rather than denouncing it as primarily anti-God, and working for a spiritual revival which will counter it.

Caliber and Conviction

Yet the Lord's word through Ezekiel to Israel and presumably to those who find themselves in similar circumstances was, "And I sought for a man among them that should make up the hedge and stand in the gap before Me for the land that I should not destroy it; but I found none" (22:30). One can hardly miss the fact that God is prepared to bring judgment to bear on the society and the individual who rejects Him, and part of the judgment is living with the consequences of the sin committed.

However, God insists that He will avert judgment when people turn to Him from their sin or "from idols to serve the living and true God" (1 Thes. 1:9). The way to bring this about is to find rugged, committed individuals who have recognized their individual sin and responsibility, repented and been forgiven, and in glad response to the call of God, have come to a place of ministry before God on behalf of the people. God still looks for the "man in the gap." Webster's definition of the phrase, "to stand in the gap" is "to expose oneself for the protection of something; to make defense against any assailing danger."

While Ezekiel didn't have the advantage of Webster's admirable erudition, there is no doubt that he understood exactly what kind of person the Lord was seeking because the succinct description He gave is full of challenging details concerning the caliber and conviction of the person God required.

Before we get into details about this, I must ask the women readers to forgive me if I, like Ezekiel, use the masculine third person singular pronoun to describe the person in the gap. This is not intended to suggest that either the Lord, Ezekiel, or the present writer believes that only a person of the masculine gender can serve God effectively. Both Scripture and history clearly teach otherwise. In fact, I have to admit that many women today seem more ready to adopt the "gap" role for God than some of the men.

Among the People

First the Lord stipulated that the man in the gap must be "among [the people]" (22:30). There is a sense in which those who would serve God effectively need to know how to withdraw from the crowd and meet with God. But at the same time, those whom God uses in society are usually those who have the ear of society and to some extent, have earned the respect of society.

Note I did not say the *agreement* or *support* of society, but the *respect* of society. The vast difference between support and respect has not always been clearly understood by those who would serve God. Often in our desire to be heard we have felt the need to be accepted, yet the fact of the matter is that if we stand for what God says to a corrupt world, we can no more expect to earn its accolades than did the Lord Jesus!

We can imagine the tensions involved in the life of the person God uses to turn things around. How does one maintain the balance between being remote enough from society to be distinctive, and close enough to society to be classified as "among the people"? The Church has wrestled with this problem through the centuries. At different times, in different ways, some who would serve God have withdrawn to a life of seclusion, while others have become so involved with their contemporaries that they indulged in society's sins and were engulfed in society's error. The former lost the ear of the people; the latter, the respect of the people. Both failed to be God's men among the people.

The Question of Involvement

The situation in the Church today bears strikingly similar characteristics. There are those who are so threatened by "the world" that they have nothing to do with its system or its people. On the rare occasions they make any attempt to be "among the people" they show that their concern is to get the people of the world converted through some special meetings or quick fire evangelistic approach. Having fulfilled by such activity what they fondly imagine to be their evangelistic responsibility, they retreat hurriedly to the relative sanctity of their church fellowship and comfortable existence.

Others, strongly resenting this somewhat heartless, uninvolved approach, have endeavored to relate to the people of the world on a long term, person-to-person basis, and in so doing have been subjected to the scathing denunciation of many believers and vaguely puzzled acceptance by the people they are trying to reach. The problem has been, however, that in their desire to be relevant and to relate they have sometimes jettisoned the distinctive message that "Jesus Christ is Lord" and have become swallowed up in work that is almost unrecognizable from that which is humanistic in outlook and agnostic in philosophy.

There is no easy answer to this dilemma and I believe the balance has to be discovered and maintained on an ongoing basis. However, there is one bright spot on the horizon. The Lord Jesus! He always managed to be the friend of sinners and keep Himself from sin. He was never at any moment less than involved with the people of His world and at the same time, there was never a moment when He was less than totally removed from their sin. He is the example we need to follow. His is the Spirit we need to imbibe!

The Hedge

"The man in the gap" also needs to "make up the hedge." This expression is also translated "build up a wall" or "build up a barricade." Either way, it is obvious that the person who is to have a viable ministry in a time of spiritual declension and disintegration must be able to make a positive contribution toward stemming the tide. There is no shortage of people who know what is wrong with everything, but there is a drastic scarcity of people who can say what's wrong, be strong enough to resist it, and creative enough to counter it.

Often when the Lord's people are confronted with a situation that requires a barricade to stem the tide, they seem to have little idea of what to do. True, they can condemn what is happening, shout at it, ridicule it, and even throw money at it, but it is so difficult to know how to raise up a wall against the situation. I admit that I am among this number on many occasions. I have the ability to see what is wrong, and to agree with the Christian consensus that "something ought to be done!" But knowing what to do and having the ability to do it is another question. But to admit this is not to excuse it. I believe that the time has come when more of the Lord's people must do something positive about the things that so obviously need their attention and are contributing to society's malaise.

There is no doubt that the basis of all Christian action in society must be the revealed will of God. The Christian ministry of building up "the hedge," therefore, must begin with the declaration of God's principles as they apply to the situation. But it ought to be obvious that the activity of the Lord's people must go much farther than the proclamation of what God thinks about it.

Recently I was asked to meet with a number of clergymen in the city where I minister and answer some questions they wished to present to me. They had been somewhat leery of my ministry because many of them adopted a different theological stance than mine and accordingly, had considerably different emphases in their ministry. After I had spoken to them by way of introduction, I was asked the first question.

"Can you tell me exactly what your church is doing about the social issues in our city?"

"Yes," I replied. "We are doing the same as practically every other church I have seen."

"Really?" he answered, brightening considerably. "I didn't realize that!"

"Yes," I said, "like most of the churches represented here, we are doing considerably more talking than acting!"

There was silence for a moment and then the men began to laugh somewhat ruefully for they knew that we were all more or less in the same position. They warmed to me after that and we had a great time together.

Gapmanship

Having stipulated to Ezekiel that He was looking for someone "among the people" who was able and willing "to make up the hedge," the Lord added that the person He was seeking should be able "to stand in the gap" (22:30). The expression is graphic! It gives a clear impression of someone who has the moral and spiritual caliber to take a stand in an exposed position, braving the opposition, clearly recognizing his own vulnerability, and accepting without remonstrance the expendability that his very position demands.

I think of Stephen speaking to the Council (Acts 6:8—7), Paul testifying before Agrippa (Acts 26), the apostles standing before the high priest (5:28-33), Martin Luther standing before the Diet of Worms, John Hus facing his accusers in Constance, Cranmer inhaling the smoke of his own burning shouting, "Be of good comfort, Master Ridley, and play the man!" Unknown Christians in Korea who stood firm before their Communist opponents, the countless anonymous martyrs of East Africa.

The Church has had her men and women standing in the gap, but in Ezekiel's day in Jerusalem, this spirit was lacking. The fires of commitment burned low; the pulse of moral courage beat feebly.

Martyrs

Martyrs don't intend to be martyrs. It is a serious thing to have a desire to make a career of being a martyr.

It is not so much martyrdom that portrays courage as the events that lead people to the extreme of martyrdom. Dying is not so much the problem as living the kind of life that makes people want to kill you. The killing is soon accomplished and is out of the martyr's control anyway. Someone else accepts responsibility for that.

It is the building of a life that bucks the system, challenges the status quo, and calls into question what is being accepted without question that constitutes standing in the gap. This may or may not lead to the relief of martyrdom.

The Absent Man

Sometimes one hears highly charged evangelists challenging young people to be willing to "die for Christ." This is relatively easy. The really hard thing to do is to stand in that gap, unmistakably different, challenging your society in such a way that it may or may not erupt in the ultimate reaction.

It is important that we remember what the gap-stander is expected to do while in his isolated position. God said he should be standing in the gap "before Me for the land" (Ezek. 22:30). This clearly speaks of a ministry of effective intercession as well as practical activity. There is that prayer which alone releases the power of God in a hopeless situation. Yet prayer is no substitute for the activity necessary to "build the barricade." And building without invoking divine intervention is an expensive exercise in futility.

God thought so highly of the potential wrapped in a gap-stander that He said that this kind of ministry could result in the land not being destroyed. Even at this late date, the mercy of God was still tugging at the coattails of His justice. He was still looking for a way of reconciliation without judgment. He still longed to bring the people to repentance and restore them to Himself. If only He could have found a man willing and ready to be that man. But He couldn't. I think one of the saddest statements in literature is the expression that fell from the lips of Ezekiel on behalf of the Lord: "But I found none."

Don't Care

The reason why none was to be found is not given, but knowing our own hearts as we do, perhaps a little inspired imagination may legitimately be exercised at this point.

Undoubtedly some would not accept the role of "man in the gap" for the simple reason that they didn't care enough. In the heart of every person is the tendency to believe that while society may be falling apart, there is always the possibility that when it falls apart he or she will survive the disaster. Interests and energies are directed toward ensuring the best possible situation before, during, and immediately after the disaster. Thinking in terms of the society in general is totally out of the thought pattern because it is fully extended in thinking only about personal situations and interests.

Don't Dare

Then there are always those who don't dare enough. The very idea of bucking Jerusalem society which was rotten from top to toe would be an unnerving proposition, and lots of people were prepared to be thoroughly unnerved at the prospect.

Added to those who didn't care or dare were those who wouldn't share. To become a marked person in any field of spiritual or moral conflict is to invite all kinds of demanding situations. The more demanding, the more taxing, and the more taxing, the less privacy is possible. It's a matter of sharing all you are and possibly all you've got when you get around to "gapmanship." This is much too high a price for some to pay when the rewards appear to be so elusive and the possibilities of measurable success so remote. There was no one to stand in the gap for the land before the Lord.

Some people have had a little difficuilty squaring God's statement that He couldn't find anyone to stand in the gap when Ezekiel and his contemporary, Jeremiah, seemed to be doing just that! Obviously the Lord was not counting them, possibly because He was looking for someone in Jerusalem. Ezekiel, as we know, was in Tel-abib, and Jeremiah was probably in prison.

In fact, Ezekiel was clearly demonstrating his "gapmanship." Having concluded the "man in the gap" speech, he turned to a harrowing allegory of Jerusalem's and Samaria's unfaithfulness. Using the familiar metaphor of Israel being the bride of Jehovah, he told the heart-rending story of the unfaithfulness of Aholah and Aholibah, two sisters who depicted Samaria and Jerusalem (Ezek. 23). The tone of this allegory left no doubt that Ezekiel cared.

Then one day as he was cooking in his copper pot, Ezekiel received word from the Lord that he should make a note of the "name of the day" (24:2). The day of judgment had finally arrived. Ezekiel promptly filled his pot with water and heaped bones in and around it. He built a fire so intense that the bones in the pot "seethed" and the bones around it burned (24:3-5). Then, turning to the crowd, he told them the judgment would be so intense it would burn out even the foulest, filthiest aspect of all the Lord hated. He certainly showed that He could not be accused of not daring enough!

But perhaps the most poignant glimpse of Ezekiel's ministry was yet to come. One day the Lord told him that his wife would die, yet he was not to outwardly mourn or engage in any of the usual activities of the bereaved. He was to go ahead with his business and thus be a sign to the people (24:16-17). Ezekiel responded to these heavy requirements in remarkable fashion. "So I spake unto the people in the morning; and at even my wife died; and I did in the morning as I was commanded" (24:18).

Seldom have I read or heard of such devotion to the Lord and His ministry. Ezekiel's critics are quick to charge him with being heartless and cold (24:19), but the Lord certainly didn't think that about him. He called Ezekiel's wife "the desire of thine eyes" (24:16). This was "gapmanship." The ministry of a man not afraid to share himself with the Lord to such an extent that a personal tragedy was permissible for the sake of the people.

Perhaps here more than at any other part of his ministry, Ezekiel showed why God may be having difficulty finding people who will care, dare, and share enough to turn things around.

10

Can These Bones Live?

Ezekiel 25—37

It is almost impossible for us to imagine Ezekiel's anguish the day his wife died so suddenly. He attracted great attention to himself by his failure to engage in the traditional forms of mourning and his apparent unconcern about his own bereavement. It should be no surprise to us by now that his behavior was a sign from God to the people which, at their request, he interpreted to them.

It was related to the impending calamity, but the Lord added a poignant touch by reminding the people that when Jerusalem and the temple finally fell, they and the Lord would be losing a treasure as irreplaceable and precious as the wife that Ezekiel had just lost. Furthermore, the people would be so stunned by the immensity of the tragedy that they, like Ezekiel, would be incapable of mourning. They would be numbed by the immensity of their loss.

Dread News
There was, however, one slight bright spot on that gloomy day. The Lord also promised Ezekiel that when the news of Jerusalem's eventual fall arrived in Tel-abib he would "be no more dumb" (24:27).

Ezekiel records what happened nearly three years later. "It was in the twelfth year of our captivity, in the tenth month, in the fifth day of the month" that an exhausted refugee arrived with the dread news that Jerusalem had fallen. "The city is smitten" was his simple message (33:21). Ezekiel was not at all surprised because not only had he been told to make a special note of the date on the day he did his boiling pot act, but the night before the refugee arrived the Lord had opened his mouth (33:22)—a further indication that the news was about to arrive.

There has been some debate as to why it took the refugee so long to get to Tel-abib. We know that when Ezra and his group made a similar journey from Babylon to Jerusalem, it only took them four months, but the account in Ezekiel shows that it took the refugee considerably longer. We cannot settle the controversy, but we do know he arrived and that Ezekiel immediately embarked on his first message after recovering his voice.

Rather surprisingly he used the opportunity to speak out against the few people who were left in Israel and Jerusalem after the Babylonian conquest. When they had awakened to the fact that they were the only ones left, they figured that since the land had been given to Abraham in the first place and they were his only surviving heirs, the land was theirs (33:24). So they laid claim to it. There was no thought of mourning, repentance, or getting back to God. Only naked opportunism. Sounds familiar, doesn't it?

To them Ezekiel said, "No way! You will no more inherit the land lost through the sin and rebellion of your generation than your contemporaries who have just died were able to keep it" (see 33:25-29). God had no intention of allowing the unrepentant to capitalize on the judgment suffered by others who were equally unrepentant!

Living with Respectability

There was another matter that deeply concerned the prophet. Now that his prophecies over a period of long years had eventually come true, he found himself with a whole new status. He had been vindicated. Previously he had been vilified, now he was suddenly saddled with respectability! During the long years of exile his colorful, unpredictable methods of communication had been a bright ray in a dismal scene. But the people had not taken him seriously except to argue against what he said. Now he was a proven prophet. Everyone was talking about him on the street corners and the crowds were coming around to hear "the man of God."

It is startling, however, to note that even after the recent traumatic events and the clear vindication of Ezekiel's ministry, he would still be given nothing more than a superficial hearing. True, the crowds would come to him, but a celebrity will always draw a crowd. They would come in great crowds because crowds always draw crowds, but their coming to hear would not be indicative of their readiness to respond (33:31). The Lord told Ezekiel, "Lo, thou art unto them as a very lovely song of one that hath a pleasant voice and can play well on an instrument for they hear thy words but they do them not" (33:32). If Ezekiel had ever been tempted to evaluate the effectiveness of his ministry by the size of the crowds he was drawing, the Lord was making sure he was saved from any such temptation in the future. The people were coming with great enthusiasm but even though they were making appreciative noises with their mouths, their hearts were unchanged.

Numbers Game

The effectiveness of anyone's ministry is determined, from the human dimension, by the degree in which hard hearts are transformed, and from the divine dimension, by the degree in which people through the ministry come to know that "I am the Lord."

In the years I have engaged in ministry around the world, I have served in situations both small and struggling, and large and flourishing. If you were to ask me, "Which kind of ministry do you prefer?" I would be less than frank if I didn't say, "The larger flourishing ministry. I much prefer preaching to people than pews!"

But if you were to ask me, "Where do you think your ministry was the ;most effective?" I would be very reluctant to answer because I have learned from the Word of God and from experience that the real work is done in the hearts of the committed nucleus, not necessarily in the ranks of the bustling mass. According to the law of averages, there is a greater chance of a bigger nucleus and therefore, the possibility of a more lasting, far-reaching work in a larger crowd.

We must beware of polarizing on this issue as we do on so many others. Some leaders have seen the danger of the crowd and have immediately started a ministry of castigating crowds and venerating small groups. Others measure spiritual effectiveness by counting heads! What really matters is not the size of the crowd but what is really going on in the hearts of the people in the crowd. If there is a large crowd looking for entertainment, the people in charge should recognize that they may be in the entertainment ministry. If the group is small, they should recognize that they may be more self-centered than God-centered and problem-oriented than mission-oriented.

Maybe it's time for a moratorium on the numbers game and a hard look at our methodology for drawing crowds. Our fascination with the "personality cult" and our readiness to accept what is superficial in the place of that which should be life-changing and God-honoring needs prayerful scrutiny. Maybe some of us need to be reminded by the Word of the Lord that instead of being well spoken of and hearing appreciative sounds most of our lives, we should recognize that the real need is for a prophet who will speak the truth in love and who may never be vindicated as a prophet in his lifetime.

The size and popularity of a ministry is unimportant. The crying need is for men and women who are so much more concerned with hearts being moved and God being vindicated that they will be almost oblivious to the size of the crowd or the sounds from the pew. We need men and women who are in tune with heaven and wait only for the eternal "Well done, good and faithful servant."

Change of Gears

From the early part of Ezekiel's prophecy one could have gained the impression that since he was a prophet of doom, he would be out of a job once the doom fell. But a careful reading of what Ezekiel said shows that he was much more than a predictor of disaster. He was also a proclaimer of God's purposes, which were far greater than destroying Jerusalem and denuding Israel. God was committed to fulfilling His covenant with Abraham that through him all the nations would be blessed (see Gen. 12:2-3). He was still sold on using Israel as a sign to the nations of His dealings with people.

God's message of justice, therefore, was always tinged with mercy. Even in the midst of His most devastating denunciations He shows promise of glorious restoration. His intent to clear the land of His sinning people was no greater than His intention to fill it again with His submissive people.

Far from being "through," therefore, after the fall of Jerusalem Ezekiel was just shifting gears. For years he had preached disaster and suffered the hard faces and the awful rejection of his person and his message, but now that he was recognized as a bona fide prophet, he was ready to come up with a lot more predictions. But this time they would be statements full of hope and glory.

Before we get into a consideration of Ezekiel's shift in emphasis, let me remind you that he also spent a considerable amount of his time denouncing the sins of the nations around Israel. Many of these statements are found in the prophecy, and it is obvious that the Lord had things to say to those who were not His people in the special sense that the Israelites were His people. It is interesting to note the decidedly uncomplimentary things He said to Tyre (26—28:19) and Sidon (28:20-24) to the north, Ammon (25:1-7), Moab (25:8-11), and Edom (25:12-14) to the east, Egypt way down south (29—32), and Philistia to the west (25:15-17). He hit out in every direction and challenged the nations that surrounded Israel!

Again there is no question of Ezekiel's courage or the universal concern of the Lord. As the servant spoke against the lands surrounding his own, the Lord was demonstrating His involvement in lands north, south, east, and west of His own people.

Note, however, that nothing is said about Babylon. Some suggest that discretion got the better part of Ezekiel's valor at this point. Others think that the expansive treatment given to Tyre was probably a thinly veiled reference to Babylon. But we must return to Ezekiel's message to Israel.

A Matter of Interpretation

So far we have run into few problems of interpretation concerning Ezekiel's statements. All his prophecies about Israel in general and Jerusalem in particular did take place and we have the great benefit of adding our knowledge of history to our interpretation of the Book of Ezekiel. From this point on, however, things are somewhat different because Ezekiel's message now relates to the future of him and his people. The big question is: How far in the future?

At first it may appear that this is a purely academic question and as we are not primarily concerned with the academics of Ezekiel's work, we can ignore the question and it will probably go away. Some think it would be nice if we could and it would, but we can't and it won't.

The problem facing all readers of prophetic Scripture is to know whether the events predicted by prophets were fulfilled in the years immediately following the prophecies, whether they were fulfilled in the coming of Christ, or if we are to look for some future fulfillment. Unfortunately, Christians have sometimes divided and even polarized on these questions instead of coolly and calmly allowing for some differences of understanding. Let's try to be cool and calm as we move on into a closer study of the prophecy.

Shepherds

At the Lord's direction, Ezekiel began to speak forcibly to the "shepherds of Israel." He charged them with the crime of ignoring the flock and feeding themselves. As a result, diseased sheep had died, the wounded had been untended, the wandering had been lost, and the flock decimated. Meanwhile, the shepherds had continued in their selfish way of life while the sheep were gobbled up by the wild beasts (34:3-6).

The Lord announced that because of their failure to function properly, the shepherds of Israel had been relieved of their duties and they would not be replaced by earthly shepherds. The Lord Himself would accept full responsibility for His sheep (34:8-10). In graphic terms He announced, "I, even I, will both search My sheep, and seek them out . . . and will deliver them out of all the places where they have been scattered in the cloudy and dark day . . . I will feed My flock, and I will cause them to lie down" (34:11-12, 15).

To a people recently made aware that they were scattered from their land and had become a prey to their enemies, the words should have been music to their ears. The promise of the overthrow of the shepherds who had failed and the promise that the nation would be restored to the beloved land was a delightful change from the messages they had been hearing for so long. Instead of whirling swords, boiling pots, dirges, and lamentations, Ezekiel was treating them to a picture of satisfied sheep feeding and resting in peace and tranquility.

However, the Lord did add that He would be separating the sheep from the goats and would still be dealing with those who had abused His sheep (34:17-22), but the general message was one of hope and encouragement.

The Lord became more specific as He explained how He planned to take over from the earthly shepherds. "I will set up one shepherd over them and he shall feed them, even My servant David . . . and I will be their God and My servant Dav d a prince among them" (34:23-24). He went even further and explained that when these things were in reality true the land would be fertile, the people would be thriving, and there would be "showers of blessing" (34:25-31).

This remarkable turnaround in the affairs of Israel would be designed, of course, to show from another perspective the majesty of the Lord. This time a Lord of restoration.

In a special way, the restoration of God's scattered people to their land would be a counterbalance to the terrible things His people had done. They had continually brought His great name into disrepute, but He would see that through His action alone His name would be shown among the nations in its true glory. He would be seen to be the God who had washed His people clean and given them a new heart and a different spirit. Those who saw it would be confronted once again with the splendor of the Lord. A Lord of forgiveness and blessing.

Dem Bones

To add weight to this already powerful message, the Lord then put His hand on the prophet and took him off on one of his famous "trips." This time it was to the valley of dry bones. Thanks to the spiritual, many people are familiar with "dem bones," even if the magnificent song has done little for their understanding of either theology or anatomy! The message of the vision is as spectacular as the vision itself.

In the mighty hand of the Lord, under the influence of the Spirit, Ezekiel was transported to a valley full of dry bones. He was deposited in the middle of the scattered, dried-out human remains and made to walk around and take a long hard look.

As he was taking in the details of his latest vision, the Lord asked him a very embarrassing question, "Son of man, can these bones live?" Ezekiel gave the classic answer, "O Lord God, thou knowest" (37:3), which might be interpreted in slightly more colloquial terms, "The Lord only knows."

His answer was a response of evasion mingled with reverence. He dare not say they could because humanly speaking they couldn't, yet the Lord was asking him and presumably He had something else in mind. Ezekiel had learned that if the Lord had something in mind, something was going to happen. And that something might even be a mass restoration of the dry bones. So he sidestepped the issue as adroitly as possible and told the Lord that He already knew.

"Preach to the bones" was the next thing the long-suffering prophet heard (37:4)! Of all the ridiculous things that Ezekiel had been told to do, this must rank near the top!

"What was that again?"

"I said preach to the bones."

I have read somewhere that Billy Graham tried out some of his early sermons on the alligators in Florida. I've heard of country preachers working the cobwebs out of their presentations by trying them out on the cows and the pigs. But dry bones!

You have to admire Ezekiel. Taking a deep breath he started. I have often wondered what he would have said if it had been left to him to decide. "Ahem. My dear bones. I'm so happy to see so many of you here today!" Or maybe. "As I stand before you all today, I'm thankful that I feel slightly better than you look."

Fortunately, the Lord told him what to say and he said it. "O ye dry bones, hear the Word of the Lord." (37:4) The response was phenomenal. There was such power in the Word preached that bones began to shake and rattle across the valley, clicking themselves into place so that whole skeletons were soon assembled. The boneyard was transformed into a skeleton storehouse. As Ezekiel continued to preach, sinews and muscles were added to skeletons and skin was wrapped around them. The valley was turned into a giant mortuary, full of orderly rows of cold, beautiful bodies (37:7-8).

The Wind

"Preach to the wind, Ezekiel," ordered the Lord. The prophet did as he was told and the wind blew from all quarters into the corpses, which promptly sprang to their feet and stood in line like a massive army (37:9-10).

"Lord, what's going on around here?" the prophet thought.

"The bones are the disjointed, discouraged, dried out, dismantled house of Israel, Ezekiel, but they need to know that I am going to intervene on their behalf and transform them from a boneyard into a battalion. Their dried out hopelessness will become a powerful, orderly demonstration of the mighty power of the Lord of hosts. My Spirit will invade them, I will restore them. They will live, and everyone will know that I am the Lord because once again I will have done what only I can do" (see 37:11-14).

The Broken Rod

As if this message was not sufficient to blow the prophet's mind, the Lord then added an object lesson. He told His man to take two sticks (perhaps two pieces of a broken staff or rod), identify them as the two halves of the divided kingdom, and stand before the people holding both sticks in one hand giving them the appearance of being joined together (37:16-17).

Then he was to announce that not only was the Lord committed to restoring His scattered people to the land in great power and authority, but He would do it in such a way that the divided nation would be unified under the same person who would function as the shepherd of Israel. This person was identified as the king under whose rule the people would have such a relationship with the Lord that the covenant between God and His people would really work. He would be their God, they would be His people, and everybody would know it (37:19-27).

In the midst of the nation, the Lord promised to reestablish the temple as evidence of His dwelling among them and their adherence to His principles. Once again the nation would announce to the world that the Lord was alive and well and very much in business among His people.

It is practically impossible for us to imagine the sheer impact of these promises as they were revealed to the prophet. Shattered by the people's sin and rebellion and overwhelmed by the weight of divine judgment, he was being told that the Lord would deal with such grace and power that He would bring His people from the wreckage of their own making and make of them something glorious. Not because they deserved it, of course, but simply because the Lord is gracious.

We have already said, it is easy to interpret the first part of Ezekiel's prophecy because it was fulfilled when Jerusalem fell under the Babylonian rule and the people were scattered in the Exile. We know the dates when his predictions were literally fulfilled. But the interpretation of the second part of the prophecy poses some problems. Those who have tried to deal with these problems have sometimes felt that, like Ezekiel, they were dwelling among thorns and scorpions, because the different interpretations of these prophecies have unfortunately led believers to sharp exchanges and even division and rancor.

My Servant David

Let's start by dealing with things over which there should be no disagreement. The Lord was obviously stating that His scattered sheep would be regathered under the leadership of a shepherd identified by Jehovah as "My servant David" (34:23). Changing the scene to the reuniting of the divided nation as pictured in the "two stick" talk, Ezekiel again talked about the united nation being led by "David My servant" (37:24-25). The nation restored to the land and reunited in the land is therefore clearly predicted, but the "servant David" needs to be identified.

King David, as we know, was a superb figure in the history of God's people. Under his leadership there had been great success and prosperity and he had been recognized as a man after God's own heart (Acts 13:22). His reign was regarded as a golden era when the nation was living at the zenith of her powers. After his death, things quickly deteriorated and disintegrated. David died over 370 years before the city of Jerusalem fell and the prophecies concerning the restoration were made. It is obvious, therefore, that unless we assume some kind of literal resurrection of David's body, the expression "my servant David" must be figurative.

John recorded the messages of the Lord Jesus in great detail. In one of them He said of Himself, "I am the Good Shepherd" (John 10:11). In another He said, "I am the true Vine" (15:1). Both of these expressions have their roots in Ezekiel and both of them show that the Lord Jesus regarded Himself as being the "Good Shepherd" as opposed to the bad ones and the "true Vine" as opposed to the unfaithful vine. John further showed his acquaintance with Ezekiel when, in the vision of Patmos, he heard the Lord identify Himself with the words, "I Jesus have sent Mine angel to testify unto you these things in the churches. I am the root and the offspring of David, and the bright and morning star"

(Rev. 22:16). We should have no difficulty, therefore, in seeing that the predictions made by the Lord through Ezekiel concerning the future glorious era of Israel involve Jesus Christ in His ruling, reigning role as "My servant David."

My Spirit
Then we must bear in mind that the Lord promised that the restoration to the land would be accompanied by a change of heart in the people. He had said, "I will put My spirit within you" (36:27) and "I have poured out My spirit upon the house of Israel" (39:29).

On the day of Pentecost, Peter made it clear that the spectacular events of that day were to be understood as the fulfillment of the prophetic utterances of Joel (Joel 2:28). The similarity between Joel's predictions and those of Ezekiel and Zechariah are so obvious that we can readily see that they were all talking of the same event. What God was promising Israel through Ezekiel began to be fulfilled in the advent of Jesus Christ and the outpouring of the Holy Spirit.

But can we go any farther than that? Can we say that Ezekiel was predicting a literal return to the land given to Abraham and the reestablishing of a nation under the Lord Jesus? Here the answers come from every angle that answers can come.

Literal Return to Israel?
In his book, *The Prophecy of Ezekiel* (Chicago: Moody Press, 1969), Charles Lee Feinberg wrote concerning the passage we are considering, "This chapter constitutes the acid test for those who would explain prophecy any other way than literally. It must be admitted, even grudgingly, that the chapter is speaking of a literal Israel, a literal land and a literal regeneration experience" (p. 205). But in the 1880s Milton S. Terry wrote in his classic, *Principles of Biblical Hermeneutics* (Grand Rapids: Zondervan Publishing House, 1974), "The modern chiliastic notion of a future return of the Jews to Palestine and a revival of the Old Testament sacrificial worship is opposed to the entire genius and spirit of the Gospel dispensation" (p. 437).

With the benefit of history on our side, some of us may smile at Dr. Terry's goof as we point proudly to the remarkable events of May 15, 1948 when against all the odds, the Jews who had returned to Palestine became the nation of Israel. But while the literal return has taken place despite Dr. Terry's statement to the contrary, anyone who has been to Israel knows that this return shows little of the outpouring of the Spirit or the worship of the Lord Jesus. The modern Israeli, though doing a superlative job under the most trying circumstances, could never be confused with a Spirit-filled believer in Jesus Christ. And with all due respect to Golda Meir, Moshe Dayan, and their colleagues, magnificent leaders though they are, they could never be confused with the promised "My servant David."

Wilhelm Moeller, writing about Ezekiel in the *International Standard Bible Encyclopedia* (Grand Rapids: Eerdmans Publishing Company, 1939) made the following interesting statement: "Christian theology will vacillate between the extremes of spiritualism and realism, one extreme constantly correcting the other, and in this way constantly approaching the correct middle course, until at some time in the future we will reach the full truth in the matter" (p. 1080).

Restoration

Many believers have decided that since theologians can't agree among themselves, they will just forget about the whole thing and concentrate on John 3:16. But this they cannot do with all good conscience. Though there is considerable debate about whether the new golden era under "My servant David" will be literally on the mountains of Israel and will be limited exclusively to the scattered children of Israel, there can be no debate that the restoration will be under the Lordship of Jesus Christ through the outpouring of the Spirit of the Lord.

Here all believers are confronted with superb truths concerning what God is doing in our world. He acts for His own glory among the nations that people may recognize who He is. This is something of great concern to every believer. The rule of Christ and the outpouring of the Holy Spirit are of equal concern, so whatever we may or may not think about the details of fulfillment, we cannot put them aside, but approach them with great joy to discover more of God's work among His people.

Showers of Blessing

With the preceding in mind, what can we learn from the story of the shepherds and the Shepherd, the vision of the dry bones, and the two sticks? It would seem to me that whenever Father, Son, and Holy Spirit work together, we can reasonably assume they will use discernible principles.

Therefore, whether we are talking about the restoration of Israel, revival in the Church, or regeneration for the lost, we may legitimately apply these principles. It goes without saying that we do this all the time, whether or not we recognize the fact. For example, the Lord's promise that there will be "showers of blessing" is sung with great gusto in many churches by people who don't know that God said it through Ezekiel to the exiles in Tel-abib and was talking about glorifying His Name through their restoration.

Incidentally, James McGranahan, wrote the hymn, "Showers of Blessing" at the same time Milton Terry was writing his book and had no problem applying the truth very specifically as follows:

There shall be showers of blessing,
Send them upon us, O Lord,
Grant to us now a refreshing,
Come and now honor Thy Word.

There shall be showers of blessing,
O, that today they might fall,
Now as to God we're confessing,
Now as on Jesus we call.

Without belaboring the point, let me draw attention to the fact that the hymn relates God's ancient promise to the 19th and 20th centuries. It applies the promise to the life of the Church and anticipates the answers because the Church is calling upon the name of Jesus and is preaching the Word of God!

What a joy for modern believers to know the Lord of Ezekiel who gathers His people to Himself wherever they have scattered! How wonderful to know that the servant David came as the suffering servant, the Good Shepherd who gives His life for the sheep. What a thrill to realize the extent to which this same Shepherd has taught His Church, "Other sheep I have which are not of this fold; them also I must bring" (John 10:16).

Boneyards
The one who would see the Lord at work in restoration, revival, or

regeneration needs to be conversant with Ezekiel's vision of the dry bones. There has to be the consciousness of the Hand of the Lord upon, the Spirit of the Lord within, and the Word of the Lord issuing forth. Otherwise, the dry bones stay very dead.

Many of the Lord's people don't like to think about the obvious boneyard in which they live, whether it is their church or their community, but God wants them to be aware of it. He will give a personal guided tour to any who will allow His hand to be upon them. He will show the extent of the deadness, the degree of dryness, and the aura of hopelessness that pervades the scene. Then He will ask the question you may not want to hear but will be deeply challenged to answer, "Can these bones live?" Ezekiel sidestepped the question beautifully, but that didn't faze the Lord. "Preach to the bones anyway!" were the instructions He gave.

Preach the Word

The servant of God who wants to see God honored and His people blessed had better remember that the mandate is to preach the Word. How many preachers need to be reminded of this. How many seminaries need to underline this. From the earliest days of Creation the Word of the Lord has made things happen. "God said . . . and it was so;" "God said . . . and it was so" (see Gen. 1). The writer to the Hebrews hit the same note saying, "Through faith we understand that the worlds were framed by the Word of God" (11:3).

The fact that God has spoken relentlessly and consistently except when He chose to be silent, must be in the mind of every servant of God. This knowledge should drive him to a study of what has been said and an unflinching proclamation of the Word, even to situations as unpromising as a valley full of dry bones! We may try many approaches and involve ourselves in a multitude of activities, but we will only be successful in making bones live to the degree that our activities are proclamations of the life-giving Word. Remember the Lord said, "The words that I speak unto you, they are Spirit, and they are life" (John 6:63).

Pray

"Pray to the wind, Ezekiel," was added to the instruction to preach (37:9). Ezekiel used the same Hebrew word for both "wind" and "spirit" in much the same way as the New Testament writers used one Greek word for the two English words. When we read that Ezekiel prayed to the winds which moved in the valley and brought life to the skeletons, we see another clear statement concerning the work of the Spirit. Preaching the Word in the power of the Spirit will not only make bones into skeletons, but skeletons into corpses, corpses into people, and people into armies.

Some of the Lord's servants seem to be satisfied with isolated aspects of the Spirit's work. For instance, those who are bent on organization are often quite happy to get bones into some degree of order. They love to hear the clicking and see the shaking, but fail to see that they are only producing orderly deadness. Others who are evangelistically inclined preach to the bones, pray to the Spirit, and get excited when individuals respond and become individually animated bones. But these have little muscle from sound diets and healthy exercise and no concept of being part of a body living in the confines of an ecclesiastical skin. In other areas of ministry there appears to be some degree of satisfaction with situations where there are fellowships as orderly and orthodox as a graveyard. There must be a whole ministry of bringing bones into bodies and forming them into armies for spiritual conquest.

Coping with Ezekiel

And the story of the two sticks? For God to bring from the four corners of the Diaspora those who belong to the divided kingdom would require nothing less than the genius of God. We talk about the "lost tribes" and there is considerable debate about the heritage and lineage of contemporary Jews. We're not even sure who they are, let alone where they are! Weird and wonderful theories have been propagated, some of which even go so far as to claim that the lost tribes are the British, a theory that was amended to include Americans! Ezekiel was used to "prove" this theory! The point is that God is committed to bringing about a unity among His people through restoration, revivals, and regeneration that will shake a watching world and show them once again who He is.

There is much that is hard to understand in this part of the Book, but don't let the parts that you don't understand stop you from responding to the things you can't avoid understanding! My problem over the years has been that I have trouble responding to what I do understand, and Ezekiel has given me plenty of problems living in the light of what God has shown me through him.

11

The View
From the Mountain

Ezekiel 38—44

If by this time you have not learned to expect the unexpected from Ezekiel, perhaps the things he had to say about Gog and Magog will help! After years of dismal prediction and dire prophecies of gloom and doom, Ezekiel had finally brought some exciting messages of hope and promise. He had outlined for the exiles the details of the new golden era that the Lord has in mind for His people, and while we do not know how seriously they took the message, it probably came as a welcome relief after all the other things they had heard for so long.

But then came Gog and Magog! Ezekiel received word from the Lord that he was to speak out against "Gog, the chief prince of Meshech and Tubal" (38:3) and speak out he did.

He began to give details of this prince's actions which so incensed the Lord. Gathering his considerable armies together and making a number of strategic alliances with other nations, Gog would cast his beady, greedy eye on the land which the Lord had restored to His people. After so much hassle and trouble, they would be so delighted to be back and living in peace and quiet that they would not even be taking elementary defense precautions and so would be easy prey for Gog and his gang.

God and Gog

The Lord explained that though Gog would devise his attack on

135

the people of God in his own evil mind, there were other factors to bear in mind. The Apostle John wrote about Gog and Magog falling prey to Satan who "shall be loosed out of his prison, and shall go out to deceive the nations which are in the four quarters of the earth, Gog and Magog" (Rev. 20:7-8).

Satan as well as Gog is involved in the attack on God's people, but we should not assume that this suggests the Lord has lost control of the situation. On the contrary, the Lord said to Gog through Ezekiel, "I will turn thee back, and put hooks in thy jaws, and I will bring thee forth" (Ezek. 38:4). At first it may seem as if the Lord was saying He was going to allow Satan to set Gog up so He could glorify Himself by knocking him down! Hardly the most noble of actions.

However, we must remember that Gog, like every other person tempted by Satan, has the freedom to decide what to do with the temptation. If he rebels and does evil, God reserves the right to use the evildoer for His own glory. Though Gog will be responsible for his own actions, the Eternal God refuses to sit back and watch him do what he wishes to the people of God. And while Satan works his nefarious will in the heart of Gog, the eye of God is upon him.

This is surely one of the great mysteries of the relationship between God and man and good and evil. Yet how else can we account for the reality of each unless we see man in his freedom rebelling against God and God in His sovereignty allowing man to be tempted to evil and using his evil to achieve His plans.

The way in which God will use the evil of Gog to bring glory to Himself is clearly stated. There will be divine intervention as the forces of Gog gather against the people of God. Great upheavals, described as "a great shaking in the land of Israel," will be so tremendous in impact that "the mountains shall be thrown down, and the steep places shall fall, and every wall shall fall to the ground" (38:19-20). The armies of Gog will be decimated to such an extent that the people of the land will be able to use their abandoned weapons for lumber and firewood for seven years and it will take seven months just to bury the dead (39:10, 12). It will even be necessary to form a special commission to do nothing else but search the land for the remains of the smitten army (39:14).

The result of all this is that the Lord who had shown Himself great in grace in choosing His people in Egypt when they were so weak, great in patience as they wandered in the wilderness, great in mercy as He withheld His judgment for centuries, great in holiness as He turned His back on their sin, and great in forgiveness as He restored His people to the land, will show Himself great in power as He ultimately defeats all their enemies. In other words, once again people would have the chance to know that, "I am the Lord."

Is Gog Red?

This weird and wonderful prophecy has been a bone of contention over the years among Bible students. Some reputable scholars feel that this prophecy is apocalyptic and as John B. Taylor explains (in *Tyndale Old Testament Commentaries,* London: Tyndale Press, 1969), "It is largely symbolical and at times deliberately shadowy and even cryptic." He warns that "attempts to read too much into the incidentals of the prophecy betray the ingenuity of the spectacular rather than the sobriety of the exegete" (p. 243).

Taylor felt that Dr. C. I. Scofield of Scofield Bible fame was demonstrating more speculative ingenuity than exegetical sobriety when he wrote concerning Gog and Magog, "That the primary reference is to the northern (European) powers headed up by Russia all agree. The reference to Meshech and Tubal (Moscow and Tobolsk) is a clear mark of identification" (Notes, *Scofield Reference Bible,* New York: Oxford University Press, 1945, p. 883).

Hal Lindsey in his phenomenally popular book, *The Late Great Planet Earth* (Grand Rapids: Zondervan Publishing House, 1970) in a witty and dogmatic chapter entitled, "Russia is a Gog" asks the question, "How could Ezekiel 2600 years ago have forecast so accurately the rise of Russia to its current military might and its direct and obvious designs upon the Middle East, not to mention the fact that it is now an implacable enemy of the new state of Israel?" He then answered his own question, "The answer is again, it seems to this writer, obvious. Ezekiel once again passes 'the test of the prophet' " (p. 66).

God Will Triumph

Again we find ourselves in the position of speculating on the degrees of fulfillment of God's Word through His prophet. Some believe a literal fulfillment means invasions of Israel by Russia and allies from North Africa and Iran. Others see the prophecies as symbolical of God's ultimate protection of His people against all the unnumbered forces of evil. Feinberg disagreed saying that translations other than literal translations should be classified as "liberties in interpreting the plain statements of the prophetic scriptures" (*The Prophecy of Ezekiel*). But H. L. Ellison, in *The Old Testament Prophets* (Grand Rapids: Zondervan Publishing House, 1966) wrote, "While dogmatism is out of place, he would be a bold man who would categorically deny that we are seeing the beginnings of fulfillment today" (p. 112).

Let me suggest several things to you who have been intimidated by the learned pronouncements of prophetic scholars.

First, don't give up trying to understand what God was saying and is still saying. As far as Gog is concerned, God will be ultimately vindicated in a final triumph over all the hosts of evil. Of that there is no doubt, and on that all prophetic scholars agree.

Second, keep a keen eye on world events. Lindsey may or may not have been right when he wrote, "Since the restoration of Israel as a nation in 1948, we have lived in the most significant period of prophetic history. We are living in the times which Ezekiel predicted in chapters 38 and 39" (*The Late Great Planet Earth*, p. 62). Watch with keen interest the maneuverings of the forces of the nations of the world. Be interested in Israel and her relations to other nations, but don't get alarmed if all the predictions of the Bible scholars don't work out exactly as they suggest or even insist. That God will ultimately intervene and overthrow all evil is beyond doubt and not even open to debate.

It's Been a Long Time

Perhaps we have been so busy thinking about Russians and Iranians and wondering about Gog and Magog that we have forgotten that Ezekiel was still in his little house in Tel-abib. In fact, by this time he had been there a long time.

If he had been captured when he was 25 and received his first great vision when he was 30, he was 50 by the time he received the final visions recorded in this book, and had lived half his life in captivity. He had spent 20 years of extremely difficult ministry.

According to this chronology, the people in Tel-abib had heard nothing for 12 or 13 years following the fall of Jerusalem. The

Lord's last words had concerned the future golden era that would begin when the dry bones came to life again. What went on in those years we have no way of knowing, but I imagine there was a lot of grumbling and questioning. Perhaps the people of those days were not so afflicted with the modern disease of immediacy as we are, but nevertheless, I feel sure that Ezekiel must have had plenty of visits from the elders and the "not so elder" inquiring about what was going on.

Delays are dreadful for people who have little concept of eternity. Waiting is something that few people like to do, yet again and again we find in Scripture that God moves more in terms of millenia than minutes. He never seems to be in a hurry, but He always gets done what He wants done! I find this to be one of the greatest areas of dissimilarity between God and the people who are made in His image. Like the Pennsylvania Dutchman we have to admit, "The hurrieder I go, the behinder I get." But God has no problem in doing nothing climactic for 12 or 13 years and sees no necessity to rush into speaking about eternal matters until He's absolutely ready to speak!

The Final Trip

Ezekiel was probably highly relieved when one day he experienced the old familiar sensation of the "hand of the Lord" upon him (40:1). The vision we are about to share with Ezekiel lasts for nine chapters and we don't get to see or hear from him again other than in his visionary state.

He was "transported" to the land of Israel and placed on a very high mountain from which he could see to the south something he described "as the frame of a city." As he stood alone on the mountain, looking across to the city, he was confronted by a man "like the appearance of brass" who was carrying a measuring line made of flax and a measuring rod just over 10 feet long. He gave Ezekiel instructions to watch carefully, listen attentively, and digest thoroughly all he was going to be shown in order that he might explain it all to the "house of Israel" (40:2-4).

The Measuring Man

Then began a long, detailed, exciting exploration of the city, starting with the surrounding wall which was about 10 feet high and 10 feet thick. This was confirmed by the man who carried the rod and line because he stopped to measure it as he and Ezekiel walked past. In fact, as Ezekiel was soon to discover, his new friend had a real thing about measuring everything! The wall had a great gateway through which they passed, and which they duly measured. They found themselves in a large courtyard (40:5-6).

While the man rushed around measuring everything, Ezekiel tried to remember all he had been told to remember. The width of the pavement, the number and size of the cells for the Levites, the distance from the outside wall to the gateway into the inner court.

His mind buzzing with details, Ezekiel followed his guide across the outer court, up eight steps and through the gate leading into the inner court. When everything was measured and recorded, they had time to look at the special furniture in the gateway. There were eight tables made of hewn stone designed for the sacrificing of animals and four more similar tables on which were kept the implements needed for the sacrifice. After inspecting the quarters of the priests who handled the sacrifices, Ezekiel was led past the altar in the middle of the inner court to the steps leading up to the temple (40:7-43).

The Temple

Ezekiel noted there were 10 steps and that the temple was divided into three sections called the porch, the holy place, and the Holy of Holies. The measuring man pointed out that the farther he went into the temple, the narrower the doors became.

He checked on the size of the massive pillars leading into the porch and particularly noticed the table that stood in the Holy Place right outside the double doors leading into the Holy of Holies. This table, his guide explained, was set specially before the Lord.

The inside of the temple and the double doors were decorated with carved figures of cherubim and palm trees. The cherubim bore the faces of a man and a young lion. The Holy of Holies, which he could not enter, was in total darkness, but the porch and the holy place derived light from windows set high in the wall. Read the detailed description of Ezekiel's tour through the temple in Ezekiel 40:44—42.

The Glory of the Lord

Ezekiel and his guide walked and measured till having looked at and measured every cubit of the structure, Ezekiel was led by his tireless guide to the gate in the outer court that faced east. To his inexpressible joy, Ezekiel saw something he had longed to see for over 19 years. The glory of the Lord which he had so vividly portrayed in his first vision and which to his horror he had seen depart from the temple, was once more appearing in the eastern sky. Nothing was different about the eternal glory (Ezek. 43:2).

Ezekiel fell on his face as he was again overcome with the sense of the presence of the Lord. The old familiar brightness was there; the sound like the rushing waters filled his ears. Once more Ezekiel knew that the Lord who changes not, was ready to enter the temple where He longed to dwell among His people (43:3-4).

Ecstatic, Ezekiel was led by the Spirit into the inner court where he gazed on the transformed temple. It was no longer just a beautiful building, but a vehicle for the living God, a vessel for His presence. For the moment he forgot about cubits and hand breadths and revelled in the glory and immensity of the God who lives. God—immeasurably greater than man's measurement, grander than the greatest design of the most ingenious person. God of gods. This God Ezekiel worshiped, for once more the Lord was visibly among His people (43:5).

The Lord Speaks

As soon as the glory of the Lord had moved into the temple, the Lord called Ezekiel and spoke to him as the measuring man stood beside him (43:6).

The burden of the Lord's heart was readily discernible. Describing the temple as the place of His feet and His throne, He insisted that the people of Israel would defile it no more. In the past they had repeatedly done this but Ezekiel was to show the detailed plan of the new temple and point out to them the specific ways in which it had been designed so that it would not be defiled in the future (43:7-12).

The Lord then began to talk like the measuring man. He went into a discourse on the size and shape of the altar. It was to be built on a solid base in three square tiers. The bottom one was to be sixteen cubits square. The middle one fourteen cubits square and the top one twelve cubits square. At each corner were the horns to which the sacrifices were tied and the blood of sacrifice was sprinkled (43:13-18).

Steps were to be built leading up to the altar on the east side. This is particularly interesting because in His earlier dealings with His people, God had forbidden steps to be built on the altar. Also note that because the steps were on the east side, the priests would have their faces to the west and their backs to the east when engaging in their duties (43:17). A total reversal from the days when they bowed toward the sun as it slowly rose in the eastern sky!

Details followed concerning the sacrificial consecration of the altar which would take seven days and much blood sacrifice to complete. After that the altar would be ready for regular daily sacrifice. Burnt offerings and peace offerings were to be part of the worship activities, speaking quite clearly of God's desire to meet with His people as they came to Him cleansed, forgiven, and accepted.

Was Ezekiel Bored?

Thinking as we do with our Western minds, we probably imagine that Ezekiel was as bored by all this detail as we are. But nothing could be farther from the truth. Ezekiel reveled in the meticulous detail and understood the deep significance his training as a priest had taught him to appreciate.

When the Lord made special mention of the priests of Zadok who would have particular responsibilities for the offerings and the administration of the altar, he was no doubt delighted. He listened carefully as the Lord outlined details of the life-style of these priests. They were to wear only linen garments when they ministered before the Lord because to sweat before the Lord was to be ceremoniously unclean! They were to change their clothes whenever they went near the people. They were given strict instructions about their hair length, their drinking habits, and their love life. They were to keep away from all corpses except those of relatives, observe the Sabbath meticulously, and act as judges in areas of controversy. They were to be supported by the people with the first fruits of their produce, and their living quarters were to be carefully located in the place of God's choosing (43:19; 44:9-31).

The Shut Door

Before receiving all this information from the measuring man and the Lord, Ezekiel was probably relieved to get a breather. He was taken into the outer court to the gate through which the glory of the Lord had entered, and he found it shut. No doubt he was surprised to see this, but the Lord explained that the gate had been made holy because the glory of the Lord had entered through it and nothing that might defile the gate again should be allowed to happen. Furthermore, no strangers "uncircumcised in heart nor uncircumcised in flesh" were to be allowed to enter the sanctuary showing once again that the Lord was serious about the preservation of the holiness of His temple (44:1-9).

What did this mean to Ezekiel? Remember that Ezekiel was still a captive of the Babylonians in Tel-abib. He was experiencing a vision of the Lord after the long silence that followed the exciting promise of restoration to the land. So there can be little doubt what all this meant to him. He was being shown that God's purposes for His people were that He should once again rule and reign in their midst. The people were to be a willing, thankful people, deeply aware of their own sinfulness and wonderfully aware of God's holiness. They were to be a people grateful for the access they had to their holy God through His chosen sacrifices, administered by His chosen servants and, no doubt, Ezekiel keenly anticipated the immediate fulfillment of all that he was being shown. With his notebook full of sketches and measurements and his mind ablaze with a fresh vision of the Lord, he was ready to tell the people about the details of what life would be like when they finally got back into the old country.

What Do You Make of This?

Is there nothing else to be gleaned from this vision? Is it nothing more than a detailed architectural plan of the temple which was to be built, a job description for priests, and a list of rules for the people? If this is the case, then we have to admit that history teaches us Ezekiel's temple never got built. True, the people did eventually return to the land and build a temple under the leadership of Ezra and Nehemiah and the verbal proddings of Zechariah and Haggai.

However, neither this temple nor the later edifice, which was destroyed by the Romans in A.D. 70, was built according to Ezekiel's design. This has led some people to say that it doesn't really matter that the temple was never built literally, because things don't always work out in practice the way they are supposed to do in theory.

Stephen Winward writing in his book *A Guide to the Prophets* (London: Hodder and Stoughton, 1968), said concerning Ezekiel's vision, "Here we have an ideal picture of the temple, community, and land. Does this mean that these visions were ineffective and futile? No! In human life, even at its best, there is always a gulf between the ideal and the actual, between our highest aspirations and our best achievements" (p. 163). He then went on to say that Ezekiel's vision and idealism had greatly influenced and encouraged the people and had even been taken up by John in his Patmos vision and used to inspire people to see the wonders of eternal life promised to believers in Christ.

To say this is almost to imply that God's plans came unglued and that He had to scamper around and think of some way of salvaging His promises. A most undignified concept to say the least!

There are many believers, of course, who have no such problems, for they see in Ezekiel's detailed predictions plans for a temple to be built and worship to be enjoyed in a future day. Hal Lindsey wrote, "Obstacle or no obstacle, it is certain that the temple will be rebuilt. Prophecy demands it." He added, "If this is the time that this writer believes it is, there will soon begin the construction of this temple" (*The Late Great Planet Earth,* p. 56).

Feinberg also looks for a similar fulfillment and speaks enthusiastically as follows, "The more one studies the detailed measurements of the chapters, the more the conviction grows that Ezekiel was speaking of a literal plan which is meant to be literally implemented in future times" (*The Prophecy of Ezekiel,* p. 238). Any other interpretation than a literal one sometime in the future he characterizes as "hermeneutical alchemy."

Exegesis

Many "hermeneutical alchemists," however, got into alchemy because of the real problems they faced with the literal interpretation advocated by such men as Lindsey and Feinberg.

J. Sidlow Baxter wrote in his well-known *Explore the Book* (London: Marshall, Morgan and Scott, 1951), "We believe it to be a sound principle of exegesis in general that unless there is some serious objection to the literal interpretation of a passage, this should be given first preference." Baxter asks the question

"Are there, then, serious objections to our taking Ezekiel's description literally?" and answers it with a resounding "There are" (Vol. 4, p. 31). He points out that some of the objections are to be found in the sheer size of the temple and the land surrounding it. In fact, he goes so far as to say that these dimensions are "physically impossible—unless the river Jordan be moved farther east!"

It must, however, be pointed out that he arrives at these conclusions by assuming that those passages which speak about "five and twenty thousand in breadth" refer to "reeds" while other commentators assume "cubits." Actually, neither is mentioned in some places! As a cubit is approximately 1½ feet and a reed is approximately 10 feet, the difference is 8½ feet, which when multiplied by 25,000 amounts to a difference of almost 40 miles! Baxter has problems fitting Ezekiel's plans into the land without moving the Jordan when he needs an area 47 miles by 47 miles but there is no need to move anything very much if the measurement is 7 miles by 7 miles! Gets complicated, doesn't it?

However, Baxter goes on to show what is involved if we believe there will be a reinstitution of the sacrificial system under the priesthood in a temple denying access to certain people who are "strangers." His comments on this are worth repeating. "Is it thinkable that after the one perfect sacrifice of Christ there should be, in the yet future temple, a reversion to these? Does not such an idea insult the New Testament?" (*Explore the Book,* vol. 4, p. 34)

More Thorns and Scorpions

It seems that if we accept the predictions as being literal, we run the risk of insulting the New Testament. But if we don't accept them as literal, we are hermeneutical alchemists! If we try to see how all the pieces fit together we may be charged with speculative ingenuity but if we fail to do this, we may be regarded as somewhat suspect. Thorns and scorpions are certainly the lot of those who would interpret Ezekiel's work!

Apocalypse

There is, however, another approach which ought to be mentioned. John Taylor feels that it is a mistake to view the final chapters of Ezekiel's book as a prophecy in the strict sense of the word. He says that this part of Ezekiel's writing is "apocalyptic" and describes this style of writing as being characterized by "symbolism, numerical symmetry, and futurism." That these characteristics are there is plain to see. He concludes that viewing the final vision as apocalyptic, "of all the interpretations seems to take the most realistic view of the literary character of the material with which we are dealing." The significance of Taylor's theory is, however, that "the visions of the temple were, in fact, a kind of incarnation of all that God stood for and all that He required and all that we could do for His people in the age that was about to dawn" (in *Tyndale Old Testament Commentaries*, p. 253).

Some may find this approach hard to take, but numerous scholars hold similar views. One application of it can be seen in G. R. Beasley Murray's notes on Ezekiel in *The New Bible Commentary* (London: InterVarsity, 1953). Concerning the details of Ezekiel's final vision he wrote, "Their essential truth will be embodied in the new age under forms suitable to the new (Christian) dispensation. How this is to be done is outlined for us in the Book of Revelation (xxi. 1—xxii. 5)" (p. 664).

What can we make of all this? There is no doubt that some of these men are wrong about some things. And it is doubtful if any of them are right about everything. Further, it is obvious they are all agreed about some things. It is also obvious that they cannot answer all the questions to the satisfaction of the people who raise them. And by now, it should be perfectly clear that I am not about to stick my neck out like some of the esteemed brethren whose works I have quoted. But I do believe there is much for us to learn from this vision and it would be a shame if we missed it because of the differing views expressed by different people.

Let's Agree on Something!

First, we all agree that Ezekiel never had the joy of seeing the temple of the vision built or the worship portrayed in the visions actually taking place. There can be no doubt that he expected it to happen in some way, but we have no way of knowing if he was permitted by the Lord to see a future fulfillment of the vision he was experiencing.

If we are to assume, however, that the day is coming when the temple will actually be rebuilt in Jerusalem and the worship of the temple be reinstituted as Ezekiel outlined, we can see that it would be purely a reminder of the superb sacrifice once and for all offered by our Lord Jesus for the redemption of a lost world. The order of worship would also indicate not a formal adherence to rules, but an outward expression of an inward experience of forgiveness and worship in Spirit and in truth.

If some of you have too great a problem with such a literal interpretation, don't be too upset because no doubt you believe that even today God dwells among His people in the Church and that He wishes to be worshiped and adored by His redeemed, restored people in holiness and reverence. You will no doubt be thrilled to know that even though you have no literal place in the priestly line of Zadok, you belong to the priestly line of those who offer spiritual sacrifices to God and who order their lives according to the design of the Lord who requires great commitment and discipline from His servants.

There is always the chance that some of you still don't feel comfortable with either of these views and prefer to think that the temple and its worship are still in the future and will only be experienced in the eternal glory as envisioned by John in the Book of Revelation. That John and Ezekiel were kindred spirits is beyond dispute and that there are marked similarities between their visions is beyond doubt. So there should be no problem seeing a clear connection between what Ezekiel saw in Tel-abib and what John saw in Patmos if one bears in mind that both men were being introduced to eternally relevant truths which would probably never be thoroughly understood this side of eternity.

Zoom Lens

Some time ago, I saw a movie which had a remarkable opening. The first scene showed a vast, empty prairie. Slowly the camera zoomed in till the screen was full of long, waving grass. Then the camera zoomed in, and the focus sharpened farther till the head of a single prairie flower filled the screen. At that point, the first sounds came over the sound track. Somewhere a harmonica was playing. Slowly the camera pulled back till the original shot showing the open prairie was in view, but this time a tiny figure had appeared in the distance. The camera zoomed in on it to show the harmonica player riding his horse. Then the camera zoomed even closer to fill the screen with the harmonica and the weather-beaten, calloused hand that held it. It was a fascinating experience to be presented with so many closely related and yet widely divergent perspectives of the same scene. From acres of grass to one flower, to a single horseman alone in the prairie, to one hand holding a harmonica. Yet, they were all necessary to complete the picture.

Can we give Ezekiel a camera with a zoom lens and allow him the possibility that his vision was one in which he zoomed from the possibility of minute, immediate fulfillment to the coming day in which the kingdom will be established for all eternity, with a quick flash to the status of the people of Israel in their land at the end of the 20th century, while showing the outworking of God's purposes in the Israel of God, the Church of Jesus Christ?

I feel comfortable with this because as we have already seen, there is no way in which all conflicting views can be all right and it is quite unlikely that any of them are all wrong. As God has shown that He is primarily concerned with revealing Himself to and through His people as and when they live, it is important for us to see how these things apply to us today, regardless of what happened in the past and despite what will happen in the future.

There Is No Doubt

So let's agree that God loves to be among His people and to let it be known that He is there. Then let us go on to see that when He is really among His people, He insists that they adhere to His principles of behavior and activity. There is no such thing as effective spirituality without disciplined obedience.

Then let us be reminded that it is a very easy and dangerous thing to take lightly the things of God and to defile His holy place whatever and wherever that might be.

Let us never forget that God is concerned about how we go about serving Him. Remember the measuring man! He is also beautifully symmetrical in all that He does. There is no imbalance with Him.

If we can get hold of these things and put them into practice, at least we won't have time to be bored waiting to find out whether all these things are going to happen in Jerusalem or heaven. We will have lots of things to do instead of worrying about whether Ezekiel's final vision was apocalyptic or prophetic. There is nothing quite like seeing God in all His glory being revealed to my wondering eyes, despite their eschatological cataracts, and joining Ezekiel in the inner court prostrate before Him, wondering what is going to happen next. At the same time, I can rejoice in all I do understand.

By the way, in reading through this chapter I have discovered what I am. I'm a hermeneutical alchemist who unwittingly insults the New Testament while trying to exercise exegetical sobriety which sometimes comes out as speculative ingenuity. As I vacillate between believing Ezekiel's vision was figuratively literal and literally figurative, I am sometimes accused of being liberal by those to my right and conservative by those to my left. But of this I'm sure: I love Ezekiel, and I love his God even more.

12

The River in the Desert

Ezekiel 45—48

As Ezekiel stood in the center of the outer court listening to the instructions of the Lord, he heard Him begin to speak about the land and how it was to be used. Till now the talk had been exclusively about the temple and its priests and their duties as they related to the Lord who resided there. But now the vision began to expand to other things.

The land immediately surrounding the temple area was to be regarded as an "oblation" (45:1). The Hebrew word used is usually translated "heave offering," and is related to the Levitical instruction that part of the offered animal should be "heaved" or "lifted up" and given to the priests as a contribution toward their support. The Lord required that the people set aside a "holy portion of land; the length shall be the length of five and twenty thousand and the breadth shall be ten thousand" (45:1).

As we saw in the last chapter, there have been some problems with this passage because the original text does not specifically state whether cubits or reeds are intended, but it is generally accepted that the distance was measured in cubits.

Land Levy
You will be relieved to know that the people were not required to lift up all that land and heave it around! But they were to regard it as a levy to the Lord! Immediately to the north of this piece of

land, they were to make a similar piece available to the Levites—the people doing the more menial tasks of the ministry. To the south of these two sections another piece half the size of the other two was to be made available for the city and its suburbs in which people representative of all the tribes should be free to live.

Thus there was to be an "oblation" of a piece of real estate about eight miles square, divided into three main sections. The most northerly piece measuring eight miles from east to west and just over three miles from north to south was for the Levites. The center piece of identical dimensions was for the priests, and the southern section measuring eight miles from east to west and a little over one and one-half miles from north to south was for the city.

Another item of importance was that the temple area in the middle of the center section was to be enclosed in a kind of buffer zone separating it from the area in which the priests would live. (See Ezekiel 45:1-6.)

The Prince's Portion

Land to the west and east of this eight-mile square piece of land was to be donated to the prince. This meant that he was given land stretching on the west from the Mediterranean to the edge of the special zone already described, and to the east the land stretched from the Jordan River to the edge of the special zone. Unlike many of his predecessors, the prince was to be satisfied with these generous pieces of property and not exercise all kinds of tyranny on the people particularly in the area of taking their land from them (45:7-8).

The order in this layout is easy to see and the significance of it is not difficult to grasp. The temple area was to be separated from all "secular" areas of activity and experience by the simple expedient of isolating it geographically from such influence. It was to be surrounded by the priest's property which, in turn, was surrounded by property given either to Levites, the prince, or the city and its suburbs, all of which was specially donated for the work of the Lord. Holiness was to be the watchword of the temple and its environs.

However we look at the details of the vision, whether on the grand scale or the minute scale, there is a tremendous sense of God showing Himself among His people. Approachable, yet distinct from His people; with them, yet totally "other" to His people.

Take a Walk

Imagine, if you will, walking with Ezekiel toward the south from a point approximately four miles north of the temple. First you would pass through three miles of territory specially devoted to the Levites who worked in the temple in the service of God. Then you would move into the priests' zone. Here you could not help noticing the unique appearance of the people, their characteristic life-styles, and their commitment to the service of the temple. After about a mile and a half you would approach the buffer zone surrounding the temple area, on which nothing was built and nothing was cultivated. A clear expression of the separateness of the temple even from those whose lives were committed to its service.

Then, approaching the solid walls surrounding the courtyard you would ascend seven steps, pass through the massive doors of the north gate, through the threshold and the porch, and past the guard rooms before coming out into the light of the outer court. Immediately in front of you would be the wall surrounding the inner court which you would approach through another gate set in the wall. To go through this gate, you would climb eight more steps.

As soon as you had passed through the gate, you would be confronted with the great altar raised high on its massive foundations, its horns reaching for the sky. Turning to your right, you would approach the temple itself, raised on a platform reached by 10 more steps. The pillars and the carved doors would tower above you as you make your way into the vestibule, then through narrower doors to the Holy Place where the table of the Lord would block the way through an even narrower door into the Holy of Holies where you could not go.

High and Holy

This journey would impress upon you how high and holy is the Lord of Hosts and yet how wonderfully approachable He is through His ordained method of the sacrificial system and the shed blood. You could not avoid being impressed by the solemnity of entering the Lord's presence. There is no way that you could have passed through all that territory bringing into His dwelling-place anything that would defile it. This was the impact of the Lord's message to Ezekiel.

His previous temple had been defiled. The priests had worshiped the sun; the women had mourned over Tammuz; the elders had worshiped the creeping pagan deities in the temple of the Lord. Never again would this happen. The Holy One of Israel had made clear that He would not be anything less than the totally Holy One in their midst, and only those who would approach Him as such would be given the chance to come into His presence.

There is great truth for us in the Lord's words to Ezekiel. There is so much that is secular in the area of the sacred, so much that is unclean in the presence of the Holy One. We lack a sense of the holiness of God and avoid any thought of the solemnity of God. Church has to be fun and soothing. The fellowship of believers must be related to our needs even to the exclusion of waiting on the Lord Himself. The Marthas who bustle are revered in the Lord's presence far more than Marys who sit at His feet and worship Him. Knowing Him takes second place to knowing oneself in much of contemporary Christianity. Grappling with the intricacies of the human psyche appears to be much more meaningful than grasping for an understanding of the divine being.

We need more "buffers" to help us differentiate between what is permissible and what is inadmissable, more "steps" to lift us from the realm of the mundane into the presence of the Lord, more "altars" to confront us with the sinfulness of sin, more "pillars" to turn our eyes above, more "gateways" to quiet our hearts in His presence, and a "Holy of Holies" where we enter only through His shed blood.

Meet the Prince
Earlier you were introduced to the prince who would be given land to the east and west of the real estate given to the Lord. He was to receive a large piece of property in this deal. In addition, he had special privileges and great responsibilities. For instance, he was allowed to use the eastern gate that had been closed since it had been used by the Lord when He returned in glory. Not that he was able to open it, but he could enter it from the west and use the facilities of the rooms in the gateway. There he would "eat bread before the Lord" (44:3).

His major responsibility was to administer the sacrifices. He was not a priest, so he was not allowed to enter the inner court, but he was permitted to stand in the eastern gate leading into the court. This gate was closed each working day but was opened for each Sabbath Day, new moons (the first day of the month), and on the special feast days. Sacrifice would be made for him and then the sacrifices for which he was responsible would be made for all the people. They would be required to give toward these offerings on a proportionate basis a portion of their flocks and oil (45:17—46:18). Then the sin offerings, meat offerings, burnt offerings, and peace offerings would be made.

Differences

Scholars have alerted us to the fact that the feasts and sacrifices Ezekiel saw in his vision differ in numerous ways from those that Moses had passed down to the Lord's people. For instance, Moses required daily offerings both morning and evening, but Ezekiel spoke only of the morning sacrifice. The Sabbath offerings required in Ezekiel's visions were more than triple those required under the Mosaic system. Ezekiel made no mention of the celebration of the Feast of Weeks, though he did speak of other major feasts. Furthermore, it is indeed strange to see that in Ezekiel's temple there is no high priest. Dr. Carl F. Keil, a highly acclaimed Old Testament scholar, saw great significance in these changes and discussed them at great length at the conclusion of his masterly study of Ezekiel.

But we must return to the prince whom we last saw standing in the eastern gateway watching the preparations for the sacrifices! It should not surprise you that Bible students are not agreed on the identity of the prince. There is a tendency to jump to the conclusion that he is the Messiah, but this cannot be the case. The prince is not a priest, needs offerings made for his sin, and has sons to whom he may bequeath his lands.

Taylor sees in Ezekiel's mention of the prince a reference to the pre-exilic idea of the priestly status of the king. He points out, though, that the status enjoyed by the prince is far inferior to the status of the kings and princes before their awful abuse of power before the exile (in *Tyndale Old Testament Commentaries,* p. 270).

Feinberg, however, is not free to identify the prince in this way because of his conviction that everything in the vision is to be understood literally. He feels that the prince is a special representative of Messiah (*The Prophecy of Ezekiel,* p. 258), while Keil, in *Old Testament Commentaries* (Grand Rapids: Associated Publishers and Authors, Inc., n.d.) states with great candor, "We are not able to detect any Messianic elements." He concludes that "these points of detail apparently belong merely to the individualizing of the matter" (p. 384).

Someone is going to have a red face about the prince one of these days! But we can be safe in saying that if he is a real person, he serves the living God in a strategic role. If he is not, he is certainly a striking figure of what it means to be the right person in the right place, gladly accepting the appointment of God with its great privileges and massive responsibilities.

Temple Traffic

Before we leave our consideration of these aspects of the temple, let us look at two other interesting touches that were revealed by the Lord.

First, He explained how the people were to enter the temple area. If they entered by a certain gate they were not free to depart through the same gate but they must cross the area and leave through an opposite gate (46:9). This shows the Lord's great attention to detail and can remind us that when we organize the affairs of the house of God, we need to be concerned about such matters as traffic patterns and other nonspiritual items! They are not really "nonspiritual," because the way in which people are either facilitated or frustrated in their attempts to attend a place of worship will have a great bearing on their attitudes when they finally get around to worshiping. Practical details such as these are thus important.

I'm sure the temple area was a hive of activity at certain times of day and particularly on the feast days. If people couldn't get near the place because all the exits and entrances were blocked, they would probably either get in a fight or go home. I say this because I have seen both happen in our church parking lot! In fact, one of our deacons has made the profound statement that "church growth in America is directly related to parking facilities!" I'm not sure about that, but I do know that Christian attitudes are more likely to become unchristian in a parking lot than anywhere else in the facility!

Fair Deal

Then there was the matter of weights and measures. The Lord had been greatly perturbed about the fact that people were being "ripped off" by merchants because their standards of measurement were as suspect as their standards of morality. The Lord made it quite clear that their spirituality was going to show in their business in a very practical way. He gave instructions that in the future they would give the people a fair deal which was going to be a new experience for all concerned (45:10)!

However you look at these sections of the vision you come up with some down-to-earth truths. It's good to know that things will be organized in the millennial temple so that all can get a fair chance of worshiping, and it is also good to know that nobody will be getting a raw deal. If you're not expecting to spend a millennium in Jerusalem, you can be sure that the Lord is prepared to see His people getting into this kind of practical Christianity without even needing a millennium! And if you see a picture of heaven in all this, you will not be disappointed to learn things will be orderly and just there! It is surely something to look forward to.

After all this detailed information, it almost seems as if Ezekiel was losing his touch. It has been a long time since he came up with something weird and wonderful in his visions. He's been so busy worrying about linen breeches for the priests, real estate, and traffic control that his vision seems to be in danger of becoming earthbound. But have no fears because the next scene of the vision is right back to the realm of the "way out."

Trickle on the Threshold

When he eventually got back to the inner court and looked toward the temple, Ezekiel saw water trickling from the right side of the threshold, down the steps, and across the courtyard on the south side of the altar. The measuring man, whom you have perhaps forgotten by this time, led Ezekiel away from the temple building through the north gate into the outer court and then hurried him to the closed east gate. When they arrived, they saw the waters running out of the temple court down the steps and heading toward the east (47:1-2).

You may be thinking, "What's so weird and wonderful about water running from under the door and across the yard? That happens every time we get a burst pipe!" Ezekiel's temple had no pipes! That's part of the mystery!

As Ezekiel stood looking at the water, the measuring man took his rod and measuring line and started rushing along the edge of the running stream till he had measured 1,000 cubits. "Wade across, Ezekiel, and see how deep it is." Our long-suffering hero did as he was bidden and discovered that the water was already ankle deep (47:3).

By the time he had returned to the bank, the measuring man was already downstream measuring furiously. Ezekiel caught up with him at the 2,000-cubit mark and was told to jump in the water again. He did as he was told and discovered that the waters were now knee deep (47:4).

The measuring man didn't wait for him until he had measured the 3,000 cubits and then as Ezekiel suspected, he had quite a struggle wading across because the trickle had become a waist-deep river (47:4). After all this, he was required to go another 1,000 cubits downstream and take yet another dip. He went straight under and when he finally surfaced he found himself caught in a current of water too strong to swim across (47:5).

The measuring man shouted out, "Son of man, hast thou seen this?" (47:6) Ezekiel's reply isn't recorded, but I have a feeling that with water pouring out of his assorted orifices, he didn't have to explain too fully that he was deeply acquainted with the river!

Strange Things

Measuring man helped him out of the water, or Ezekiel having spent all those years in the desert, might have drowned symbolically in the river. Surely an ironic demise!

As they returned together along the bank, Ezekiel noticed that all kinds of trees had grown profusely on both sides of the river. The measuring man explained to him that the river which disappeared from their view actually flowed to the Dead Sea by way of the desert. This remarkable statement was made even more remarkable by the explanation that when the waters reached the Dead Sea, it would lose its deadness and become a veritable fish tank. Fishermen who normally didn't even bother to look in the salt-laden Dead Sea would discover to their delight that the fish were there for the taking in great quantities. But there would be some marshy places that would not be touched by the river and would simply remain salty (47:8-11).

Ezekiel continued to be fascinated by the trees which were growing in the strangest way. He was informed that they would bear high-protein fresh fruit and that their evergreen foliage would have medicinal properties. When he asked how all these remarkable things could possibly happen, he was simply informed, "Because the waters issue from the sanctuary!" (47:12)

Tribes

After the river trip, the Lord gave more details about the geographical limits of the land and its apportionment among the tribes. They were all given their own particular territory. To the north of the "levy" land, way up in the northern border country, Dan was to get a slice of territory stretching across the land from east to west. To his immediate south came Asher, Naphtali, Manasseh, Ephraim, Reuben, and Judah. This meant that Judah's territory bordered on the special Levites' area. Down in the deep south, Gad had his piece of property. On his northern border was Zebulun, then Issachar, Simeon, and Benjamin. This placed Benjamin immediately south of the designated border of the city (47:13—48:9).

If this is somewhat difficult to visualize, look at a map of the U.S. and you will see how the territories were divided in large pieces of land which we call the states of North Dakota, South Dakota, Nebraska, Kansas, etc.

Humanitarian

The Lord gave some delightfully humanitarian instructions when He reminded Ezekiel about the "strangers" among the tribes. Those who showed signs of wanting to identify with the Lord's people were to be given the same rights as the others when it came to dividing the land (47:22).

When we link this instruction with the Lord's clear words about protection of the weak against their potential oppressors and the details concerning the "year of liberty" when built-in safeguards against societal ills were put into force, we see that the Lord has always had a heart for the hurts of all people.

Followers of the Lord should never have a problem when they have to make decisions to help people in a practical humanitarian fashion. They should go right ahead to the glory of the God who does the same kind of thing!

Gathering at the River

Having roamed around the land and rambled about other issues for a little while, perhaps you feel that we should again gather at the river. We do need to spend more time looking into this truly phenomenal feature of Ezekiel's vision.

First let me point out what is probably already quite obvious. This river was no ordinary river! It got progressively deeper very quickly which is most unusual, but when we consider the fact that it had no tributaries, we can see that this river was unique. Rivers don't get deeper without input from other sources. This river not only had no other sources, it could not have any because the secret of its effectiveness was its sole source in the sanctuary (47:12).

We should also bear in mind that it started life as a trickle under the door of the temple which was situated on top of a mountain. Now rivers don't do that kind of thing. Furthermore, the trees which had such miraculous capabilities were totally dependent on the river, so we have no problem seeing that the river was unique.

Miraculous

All commentators agree that the river was unique—which is encouraging but they get back to hearty disagreement at all points west of here. Those who maintain that the vision will be literally fulfilled in the Millennium in Palestine recognize that some changes will be necessary in the geography of the country.

Dr. J. Dwight Pentecost wrote in his exhaustive work *Things to Come* (Grand Rapids: Dunham Publishing Company, 1958), "The topography of the land will be altered. Instead of the mountainous terrain which characterizes Palestine today, a great fertile plain will come into existence at the second advent of Messiah. . . . This changed topography will permit the river to flow out from the city of Jerusalem and divide to the seas to water the land" (p. 509).

If you were to question those who expect to see a literal river about some of the difficulties posed by this interpretation, they would probably answer similarly to Feinberg who states simply,

"It is miraculous. Since when has God been confined to the laws which He Himself made in nature?" (*The Prophecy of Ezekiel,* p. 271) No believer is going to challenge that argument although he might feel free to say, "I don't doubt the possibility of God doing all that but I question the probability."

Living Water

There is another side to the possible interpretation of Ezekiel's river that we should explore. Scripture is replete with references to rivers that play a monumental role in the affairs of the human race.

In Genesis there is particular mention of a river which split into four branches as it went out of Eden to water the garden. Among other things, this river watered the garden in which grew the tree of good and evil and the tree of life (Gen. 2:10-14).

The first psalm refers to the blessed man who knows what it is to counter the philosophies of his secular society by heeding the Word of God on which he meditates day and night. The psalmist says, "He shall be like a tree planted by the rivers of water that bringeth forth his fruit in his season; his leaf also shall not wither and whatsoever he doeth shall prosper" (Ps. 1:3).

The prophet Joel stated that the day would come when "the mountains shall drop down new wine, and the hills shall flow with milk, and the rivers of Judah shall flow with waters, and a fountain shall come forth of the house of the Lord" (Joel 3:18). Zechariah spoke in a similar vein about the day in which "living waters shall go out from Jerusalem" (14:8).

This immediately reminds us of the words of the Lord Jesus who promised in His dramatic speech at the Feast of Tabernacles, "If any man thirst, let him come unto Me and drink. He that believeth on Me, out of his innermost being shall flow rivers of living water" (John 7:37-38). Earlier He had told the woman at the well of Sychar that "living waters" could be had from Him for the asking (John 4:13-14).

Then in the great climactic book of the Bible containing the record of John's vision on the isle of Patmos, we read of "a pure river of water of life, clear as crystal, proceeding out of the throne of God and of the Lamb" (Rev. 22·1). Strikingly similar characteristics to Ezekiel's river and trees follow in John's beautiful description.

Life in the Spirit

There is no doubt that Scripture often uses the analogy of the river to speak of the blessings that flow to man from God. At the beginning of his history, he was in a garden where he enjoyed fellowship with God and all the fruit he needed for wholeness of life. The river nourished the trees that provided the fruit for him.

We have already seen there is life to be had and fruit to be grown when life's roots are deep into the things of God. The Lord also showed conclusively that this life comes through an experience of His Spirit which brings the full flow of divine blessing not only into, but out from, the life of the believer. John showed this river of water of life still flowing from the throne in eternity. From the beginning to the end of Scripture and I believe, from the beginning to the end of human history, there is flowing from God a river of blessing that has brought, does bring, and will bring the outflow of God to the world of man.

But like Ezekiel and the man with the measuring line, we need to take a long walk along the river. We need to see how our sin cut us off from its flow way back in Eden. We need to be reminded of our Lord's commitment to bring the flow back through His sacrificial death and the restoration of His Spirit to our barren lives. Walking along, we should again see the importance of abiding in the Word of God if the waters are to flow, and then to recognize the possibilities of the outflow like "rivers of living water."

A Deepening Experience

The river of blessing gets progressively deeper as it flows from the sanctuary past the altar. It reaches ankles and knees and loins and goes right over people's heads. Perhaps we can make an analogy. The river of blessing will flow from the believer's life when the heart is the sanctuary and the Lord is residing therein in glory. The altar of sacrifice will be in the life and the outflow will be touching people's ankles and teaching them to walk in the spirit. Reaching their knees that they might pray in the Spirit, and reaching their loins to make them strong in the Spirit as they are swept along in the fullness of His current. The magnificent thing about the Spirit's life flowing from the believer's life is when he begins to see people being caught up by the river and swept along in its fullness. Really over their heads as far as the power of the Spirit is concerned.

Personal Experience

Do you remember the question the measuring man asked Ezekiel? "Son of man, have you seen this?" Ezekiel probably felt that he had not only seen the river but swallowed half of it as well.

But could it be that the question was intended to convey the idea, "Son of man, have you experienced this?" I think this is a valid question each of us should ask ourselves as we come toward the end of this vision. Have you really known the power of the life of God so thoroughly in your life that its impact has been visible in other people's lives as well as in your own? Are they learning to walk in the Spirit as the river gets to their ankles? Are they praying in the Spirit as it laps around their knees?

These questions are the real stuff of personal evaluation. It's in these areas that we can really begin to sense the effectiveness of our spiritual life and see something of the impact of the Spirit through our lives.

Unexpected

Seeing unexpected things happen when the Spirit of God begins to work has always been a thrill and a mystery to me. Like the trees that appeared out of nowhere, blossomed, and bore their fruit continuously, so unexpected things tend to happen in superlative fashion on a remarkably consistent basis when God is at work.

So much of our life and ministry lacks the touch of the supernatural, the unique mysterious edge of the Lord. Far too often we settle for what can be produced by the predictable method and thereby rob ourselves of the thrill of seeing the trees come up from nowhere and the fruit insist on growing.

This is not to suggest for a moment that we should leave everything to chance and call it "waiting on the Lord." It does mean that if we ignore the necessity of allowing for the divine initiative and fail to leave room for the action of the Almighty, we're not really flowing on the same river as He is.

Food and Medicine

Perhaps some of the preceding concepts have been too general for some of you. You think it's fine to talk about the spiritual concepts, but what can we expect the Lord to do in our lives in real terms when the Spirit is flowing? The answer to that is that He will provide a great pile of food for the hungry and vast amounts of medicine for the sick.

I am amazed as I see the Lord taking relatively new believers and making them His agents who in a remarkably short period of time are feeding hungry people. Some people in our church don't really get too much from my preaching. They say it's either over their heads or too elementary. This doesn't really bother me, because I don't expect to be able to minister to all 2,000 or 3,000 of them. But I would be perturbed if I was not seeing many "feeders" coming along in the fellowship, and feeding the people I miss. The question I would ask you is: "Who exactly are *you* feeding?"

The Sick

There are sick people in the fellowship and around the area in which we live. Some are physically sick; others are mentally sick; all are spiritually sick. Some are mentally sick because they are spiritually sick, some are physically ill because they are spiritually unhealthy.

These sick ones need to be ministered to by the leaves from the trees. This I see happening in many lives. Wonderful, spiritual people have learned not only to diagnose the illness but can minister to the need themselves or know who can minister in the way required.

And the fishermen are busy all the time! With their nets, they stand in the teeming shoals of fish and haul them in. "Son of man, hast thou seen this?"

Fulfillment

When we go on a binge of application, we tend to forget poor old Ezekiel, but I expect he got used to being neglected! However, we should not forget that this remarkable vision was given to him while the restoration was still far away, while the dust and the bugs and the hopelessness of exile were real and unpleasant.

We have no way of knowing just what the details of the vision meant to him. In all honesty, we cannot know exactly what all the details mean to us in our day either. If we look for a Millennium in Palestine, we anticipate a miraculous situation, orderly and holy, in which there will be incontrovertible evidence that the Lord is in His holy temple. This will be a delight beyond understanding, to be surpassed only by the thought of glory a thousand times more wonderful than the most fantastic experience in this world that groans and travails and waits to be redeemed. If we see the fulfillment of the details to some degree in the life of the Church in this age, we have to admit that the fulfillment is sadl lacking the ultimate glory of the eternal state.

Nevertheless, the exhilaration of knowing the rivers of blessing today cannot be denied and must not be deprecated. The honoi of being part of the temple of God and the fellowship of believers should not be lost as we look into the future, yet we must realize that the church problems will not be ironed out till glory. Bur still the rivers and the temple and the glorious presence of the Spirit are known and revered.

Only when we finally get away to heaven will we find Ezekiel fully understanding what he saw. And guess who'll be beside him? The measuring man! And who else? John Taylor talking to Charles Lee Feinberg and Dwight Pentecost worshiping with H. L Ellison, while Hal Lindsey and Carl Keil try to figure out what was wrong with their exegesis! And way in the background you and I can take a little while to discuss the deficiencies of this book about Ezekiel.

Jehovah Shammah

How do I know all this? It's easy. The last thing that Ezekiel saw in his vision was the name of the city in which the temple was situated. Jehovah Shammah was the name; it means "the Lord is there" (48:35). And that is all that really matters. No matter how the future is unfolded to us, we will see the principles of God's revelation to Ezekiel at work. And at the very center of those principles is the Lord's personal, powerful presence. If "the Lord is there," then things will be worked out to His glory and that is the whole point of the human experience and the universal exercise. Anyone who honestly honors the Lord in spirit and in truth will experience Him at any point of his life in every detail of his life. And the ultimate experience will occur in the eternal glory which will be magnificent because "the Lord is there."

But before we get that far, who knows where else we're going to be and what else we're going to go through. Nobody really knows, but one thing we do know, whatever and wherever, we will be able to say, "the Lord is there."

What Really Matters

Differences there are in our ecclesiastical circles, and that's fine. It shows how much we don't know, keeps us humble, and gives lots of opportunities to exercise grace and patience. So thank God for honest differences among the people who gather around the place called "the Lord is there."

If it's any encouragement, let me remind you that the city called "the Lord is there" was surrounded by tribes with common ties and very obvious differences. The land was divided even there! But that doesn't really matter anymore. Once they know and we all know that "He is there," nothing else will matter.

Bibliography

Baxter, J. Sidlow. *Explore the Book.* London: Marshall, Morgan and Scott, 1951.

Ellison, H. L. *The Old Testament Prophets.* Grand Rapids: Zondervan Publishing House, 1966.

Davidson, F.; Stibbs, A. M.; and Devan, E. F., eds. *The New Bible Commentary.* London: Inter Varsity, 1953.

Douglas, J. D., ed. *The New Bible Dictionary.* London: Inter Varsity, 1962.

Feinberg, Charles Lee. *The Prophecy of Ezekiel.* Chicago: Moody Press, 1969.

Harrison, Roland Kenneth. *Introduction to the Old Testament.* Grand Rapids: Eerdmans Publishing Company, 1969.

Keil, Carl, and Delitzsch, Franz. *Old Testament Commentaries.* Grand Rapids: Associated Publishers and Authors, Inc., n.d.

Lindsey, Hal. *The Late Great Planet Earth.* Grand Rapids; Zondervan Publishing House, 1970.

Orr, James, ed. *The International Standard Bible Encyclopedia.* Grand Rapids: Eerdmans Publishing Company, 1939.

Pentecost, J. Dwight. *Things to Come.* Grand Rapids: Dunham Publishing Company, 1958.

Tenney, Merrill C., ed. *The Zondervan Pictorial Encyclopedia of the Bible.* Grand Rapids. Zondervan Publishing House, 1975.

Terry, Milton S. *Biblical Hermeneutics.* Grand Rapids: Zondervan Publishing House, 1974.

Winward, Stephen. *A Guide to the Prophets.* London: Hodder and Stoughton, 1968.

Wiseman, D. J., ed. *Tyndale Old Testament Commentaries.* London: Tyndale Press, 1969.

Inspirational Victor Books for Your Enjoyment

U-TURN A practical and relevant study of the Book of Luke, God's Gospel of New Life. By Larry Richards. Textbook **6-2236—$1.95/** Leader's Guide **6-2907—95¢**

THE ACTS—THEN AND NOW Henry Jacobsen discussed how the early Christians were, and we can be, triumphant in spite of circumstances. Textbook **6-2239—$1.95/** Leader's Guide **6-2906—$1.25**

BE JOYFUL In this study of Philippians, Warren W. Wiersbe identifies the things that rob Christians of joy, and supplies overcoming answers to such joy-stealers. Textbook **6-2705—$1.95/** Leader's Guide **6-2918 —$1.25**

BUILDING A CHRISTIAN HOME Dr. Henry R. Brandt, Christian psychologist, with Homer E. Dowdy, Christian journalist, guides Christians into mature judgments in interfamily relationships. Textbook (cloth) **6-2044** **$3.00/** Textbook (paper) **6-2051—$1.95**

GOD, I DON'T UNDERSTAND Kenneth Boa examines "mysteries" of the Bible, explores the reason for them, and explains why we must not try to solve them. Intriguing. Leader's Guide includes overhead projector masters, with instructions for making transparencies. Textbook **6-2722—$2.50/** Leader's Guide **6-2942—$2.25**

THE KINK AND I: A PSYCHIATRIST'S GUIDE TO UNTWISTED LIVING James D. Mallory, Jr., M.D., a dedicated Christian and practicing psychiatrist, with Stanley C. Baldwin, points the way to healing for those common neurotic twists that hurt all of us. Strongly Bible-based. Textbook **6-2237—$2.25/** Leader's Guide **6-2910—95¢**

HOW TO SUCCEED IN BUSINESS WITHOUT BEING A PAGAN How a Christian can run the corporate rat race without trading Christianity for paganism. By Glen Hale Bump. Textbook **6-2712—$1.50/** Leader's Guide **6-2925—95¢**

BECOMING ONE IN THE SPIRIT Larry Richards explains how oneness in Christ can find expression in every relationship of life. Textbook **6-2235—$1.75/** Leader's Guide **6-2905—95¢**

NOW A WORD FROM OUR CREATOR Leslie B. Flynn brings the Ten Commandments to life in terms of what God expects of His people today with contemporary anecdotes and relevant illustrations. Textbook **6-2728—$2.25/** Leader's Guide **6-2945—95¢**

GOOD NEWS FOR BAD TIMES A down-to-earth exposition of 1 Peter, by Richard De Haan. Encourages steadfastness and confidence in bad times because of the good news that God has chosen us in Christ, and will stand by us in life's difficulties. Textbook **6-2719—$1.95/** Leader's Guide **6-2940—95¢**

Add 40¢ postage and handling for the first book, and 10¢ for each additional title. Add $1 for minimum order service charge for orders less than $5.

Prices are subject to change without notice.

VICTOR BOOKS

a division of SP Publications, Inc.
WHEATON. ILLINOIS 60187

Buy these titles at your local
Christian bookstore or order from

B

Inspirational Victor Books for Your Enjoyment

BE REAL An excellent practical and devotional study of 1 John, by Warren W. Wiersbe. Rich in illustrations that guide students in applying truths to their living. Textbook **6-2046—$1.95**/Leader's Guide **6-2902—95¢**

THE GOOD LIFE A study of the Epistle of James, by Henry Jacobsen. Acquaints students with God's plan of salvation, and helps them find "the good life" in a personal maturing relationship with Jesus Christ. Textbook **6-2018—$1.95**/Leader's Guide **6-2930—95¢**

BORN TO GROW Larry Richards shows how to develop spiritual attitudes, new patterns of living, and a new awareness of God after conversion to Christ. Excellent for new Christians. Textbook **6-2708—$1.95**/Leader's Guide **6-2920—95¢**

THE MAN WHO SHOOK THE WORLD Biblically authentic biography of Paul, by John Pollock. Every detail of historical background is from the most accurate scholarship available and personal research in Bible lands. Textbook **6-2233—$2.50**/Leader's Guide **6-2903—95¢**

19 GIFTS OF THE SPIRIT Leslie B. Flynn discusses spiritual gifts, their purpose, and how a believer can discover and put his own gifts to use. Textbook **6-2701—$2.50**/Leader's Guide **6-2915—95¢**

WINNING WAYS Suggestions, by LeRoy Eims, on how to prepare for witnessing, approaches that can lead to witnessing, and how to witness so that people will listen. Textbook **6-2707—$1.95**/Leader's Guide **6-2921—$1.25**

WHAT EVERY CHRISTIAN SHOULD KNOW ABOUT GROWING LeRoy Eims displays a contagious sincerity and love for the Lord as he leads new believers into patterns of healthy Christian growth and discipleship. Textbook **6-2727—$2.25**/Leader's Guide **6-2947—$1.25**

THE BIBLE AND TOMORROW'S NEWS Dr. Charles C. Ryrie takes a new look at prophecy with the daily newspaper in hand. A sound, sober, and trustworthy study. Textbook **6-2017—$1.75**/Leader's Guide **6-2932—95¢**

WHAT DID JESUS SAY ABOUT THAT? Stanley C. Baldwin examines *all* Jesus said on 13 important subjects. Deals in depth with a search into their profound implications. Comprehensive, contemporary, and provocative. Leader's Guide includes overhead projector masters, with instructions for making transparencies. Textbook **6-2718—$2.50**/Leader's Guide **6-2939—$1.95**

Add 40¢ postage and handling for the first book, and 10¢ for each additional title. Add $1 for minimum order service charge for orders less than $5.

Prices are subject to change without notice.

VICTOR BOOKS

Buy these titles at your local Christian bookstore or order from a division of SP Publications, Inc.

WHEATON, ILLINOIS 60187

C